Storm
IN A
D~CUP

Storm
IN A
D~CUP

THE AUTOBIOGRAPHY OF
JUNE KENTON

The
DRIVING FORCE BEHIND
RIGBY & PELLER

B KEN

Production: SJG Gift Publishing

Cover design: Milestone Creative

Content design: seagulls.net

Printed in Poland

ISBN: 978-1-5272-0204-7

For Harold, David, Jill, Hannah, Rachel & Emily

ACKNOWLEDGEMENTS

First and foremost I have to thank my Harold. Without his love, support and companionship I would not have a story to tell.

My children, David and Jill, are the ones who encouraged me to start this adventure and I have to thank them for all their support and encouragement.

I am indebted to Daphne Gerlis for allowing me to use so much of her work from *Those Wonderful Women in Black* (Minerva Press, 1996); to the *Croydon Advertiser* for generously allowing me to reproduce their photo taken the day Sylva Zalmanson was released; to Leeds Beckett University (formerly Leeds Metropolitan University); and to Ronald G. Smith who has given me permission to use his photo of Rigby & Peller in South Molton Street. (Ron also used to help us with shop maintenance and was always known as 'Ronald McDonald', the nickname Harold gave him when we first met.) Madonna Benjamin, too, is a generous woman for allowing me to freely reproduce extracts from her brilliant documentary, *Giving the Empire a Lift*. Every effort has been made to contact the relevant people/agencies who own the copyright of the text I have quoted and other photos I have used and I am grateful for the courtesy and assistance of those who responded. (If I didn't find you, please do get in touch!)

Who, in this day and age, can live without Wikipedia? It is a resource that has saved me hours and hours of trekking to my local library so I am very grateful indeed to Jimmy Wales and Larry Sanger. Their amazing website has helped me remember so many different things that I had long forgotten.

I must also thank Clive Dickinson for his wisdom and advice; and the incomparable Fay Wrixon for all the help she has given me in gathering my thoughts.

In telling my story I have used various words or expressions that you may not be familiar with, so you can find a short glossary at the back of the book if you need it.

PROLOGUE

People say they would kill to know what I know – and that is exactly what they would have to do. I have seen some unbelievable sights and heard some extraordinary stories but, when it comes to confidentiality, being a corsetiere is a little like being a doctor.

Would I tell? Never.

And don't think for a moment that I could be tempted to share intimate details about anyone, let alone the Queen of England or any of the other royals I have served. I would rather be sent to the Tower. What I will tell you is how terrified I was the first time I went to Buckingham Palace.

It was July 1982. My husband and I had been asked to buy the made-to-measure lingerie business, Rigby & Peller, which had held the Royal Warrant to Queen Elizabeth II for more than twenty years. The Royal Warrant is awarded to a company, but within the company is a nominated person called the grantee. Tessa Seidon was the Rigby & Peller grantee and I was only interested in taking on the company if I could take on her position. She thought that it would be possible, but the extremely personal nature of our trade meant I had to meet the Queen before it could be signed and sealed.

There are no words to describe the terror I felt. Everyone is nervous when they meet the Queen. You worry about what to wear, whether your hair is right, whether you are wearing the right shoes and whether you can curtsey without falling over. And that is when you are meeting the Queen in public. I was going to meet her in her bedroom!

Once the date was set I couldn't sleep; I was a complete mess. It didn't help that I knew Mrs Seidon (I never called her Tessa) was always nervous and had never got used to fitting the Queen. I don't know how many Librium Mrs Seidon took before every visit to Buckingham Palace but still she fretted about being late.

Punctuality with the royal household is not optional. We had to be outside the Queen's bedroom at one minute to nine – not five minutes before or two minutes after – and I had been told that it took about ten to fifteen minutes to walk from the tradesmen's entrance through to the lift that takes you up to the Queen's apartments.

My wonderful husband Harold, ever supportive, did his best to calm me down and offered to drive me to the palace on the appointed day. From the moment I got out of bed everything was a worry and the journey from home into London was a nightmare. Every time the lights changed I thought I was going to have a heart attack. By the time we got to Buckingham Palace Road I was a gibbering wreck. Harold dropped me off and I found Mrs Seidon perched nervously on the edge of a chair watching the door (I was not late, she was ridiculously early).

There is nothing special at all about the tradesmen's entrance of Buckingham Palace. It is just like the tradesmen's entrance of a major department store or a grand hotel, with the exception that there is more security. I signed in, had my photograph taken, and joined Mrs Seidon to watch an assortment of workmen come and go until a footman came to collect us. This charming, quiet man led us through the vast and shabby basement area of the palace. We went past the kitchens and workrooms, through the floristry area, and finally, after what seemed like mile upon mile of corridor, into the lift that goes up to the Queen's private apartments. The footman escorted us to the waiting room.

Through the window I could see the Royal Standard fluttering madly in the wind. It looked exactly the same as it always did, but this time I was watching it from inside Buckingham Palace. Mind you, where we were sitting was not palatial at all. I had imagined gilt frames and gorgeous furniture but instead there was a jumble of mismatched, assorted bits and pieces. It looked just like an old-fashioned dentist's waiting room, which was fitting really as I was as nervous as if I was going to have all my teeth pulled out.

Just before the appointed hour, Miss McDonald came to get us. As a young woman, Margaret McDonald had been the Queen's nanny and went on to become her dresser, responsible for looking after the royal clothes and jewels. I had read that her nickname, Bobo, was the first word the Queen ever uttered, but to me she was always Miss McDonald and I came to adore her. She was a warm and friendly woman and did her very best to put me at ease. I was far too terrified to take in my surroundings and too busy paying attention to Miss McDonald's instructions to remember which way we went.

I was told that on entering the Queen's bedroom you curtsey and say, 'Good morning, Your Majesty'. Thereafter you call the Queen Ma'am (to rhyme with ham), wait until you are spoken to and never initiate a conversation. I made particular note of the last instruction as I have a well-earned reputation for talking to anyone and everyone. 'No chatting, June,' I repeated to myself over and over.

At one minute to nine o'clock precisely we were outside the Queen's bedroom door and one minute later, as the Sovereign's Piper started up on the terrace, Miss McDonald gently knocked on the door and we entered.

Every weekday morning between nine o'clock and quarter past, a piper plays outside the Queen's suite of private rooms. Queen Victoria, I believe, started the custom in 1843 after a visit to Scotland and since then, apart from a short break during World War II, there has always been a Sovereign's Piper to play outside the royal window, come rain or shine.

No sooner had we entered the Queen's room than the sky darkened dramatically and there was an enormous thunderclap. Calmly the Queen walked over and turned on the light. I don't know why I was so surprised that she did it herself because under the circumstances she could hardly have called on a footman, but I confess I was taken aback. Her Majesty then looked out the window and said that she hoped it would not rain as she had eight thousand people coming for tea. Eight thousand! I realised it was the morning of one of the Queen's garden parties and all I could think was that if I were her I would be busy cutting sandwiches rather than bothering with a bra fitting. Her Majesty's thoughts were obviously elsewhere as she ordered the dogs be brought in from outside and only then did we settle down to the business in hand.

Pipe Major MacRae's pipes were still droning when Miss McDonald ushered out Mrs Seidon and me, and escorted us back into the care of the footman. I was in a complete dream as we retraced our steps. I, June Kenton, a little (I'm only five feet two inches) Jewish woman from Croydon, had met the Queen and was walking through Buckingham Palace. I would be fibbing if I didn't say that it all felt a long way away from Brixton Market.

CHAPTER ONE

Brixton, not being in north London, was not on my mother's radar. It was the word 'market' that made her splutter. 'A market, June? Really? Harold? A market? Are you sure?'

As it happens, we were more than sure. Harold was a sales representative for women's clothing and had been supplying Manney Bonstein for several years. He knew that Manney had built up a fantastic business in two adjacent, open-fronted units in Market Row in Brixton. In one unit they sold jumpers, blouses and hosiery and in the other underwear and nightwear. Harold had always been impressed by what a wonderful business it was and now Manney wanted to sell up and retire.

It was the summer of 1961 and I had just got engaged to Harold Kenton, the kindest, most thoughtful, most gorgeous man I had ever met. We both worked for a lovely man called Phil Lee who owned a clothing wholesale company called Victor Bright Ltd in Fitzrovia, west London. While Harold was one of the reps, I was what was rather grandly called a showroom assistant, although what I really did was take orders over the phone then pack the goods ready for delivery.

It was hardly love at first sight, but Harold and I had got together (through one of his ruses which I will tell you about later) and now we were convinced that we had the perfect chance to go into business for ourselves. Harold thought that he would stay on as a rep for Phil Lee, so that we had a guaranteed income, and I could run the shop in Brixton. 'It's too good an opportunity to miss, June,' Harold kept saying, 'and besides, you know about retail.'

Harold was right. I was a Collier after all; I came from a family of retailers. My parents had owned a successful women's wear shop on Kilburn High Road for years and the retail giant Joseph Collier, or John 'The Window to Watch' Collier (named after his famous advertising slogan), was my Uncle Jock.

Mummy was a very good businesswoman but since my father's death two years earlier she had taken to turning to Jock, his younger brother, whenever she was not sure what to do. This being just such a case, Harold and I were packed off to Hampstead to tell him what we had in mind.

Uncle Jock was a very shy man but he quietly sat us down and listened attentively as Harold described the business in great detail. When Harold finally finished Uncle Jock turned to me. 'Do you realise, June, how cold it will be? Those units may have a roof and walls but in all other respects they're open to the elements. You've never been cold in your life. How will you cope?' He lit yet another cigarette. 'And what about the business side of things? If Harold's going to keep working with Phil Lee during the week, you'll be on your own Monday to Friday. Can you really do this?'

'Just watch me,' I said. Not only did I want to convince myself and everyone else that I could do it, but I was desperate to prove I had a business head on me. I had adored my father but when I worked in his shop he was always in control and I never had the chance to prove my worth. Brixton Market seemed the perfect opportunity to show that I was a true Collier.

Uncle Jock, although not entirely convinced, sent us back to my mother to discuss the all-important question of money.

Manney's asking price was eight thousand pounds. Mummy decided she would give Harold and me five thousand pounds and lend us the rest, to be paid back in weekly instalments of fifty pounds. 'Five thousand pounds is what your father and I gave Helen when she got married, so it seems only right to give you the same,' she said with a smile.

We were, of course, extremely grateful and I decided it would be ungracious to mention that my older sister had got married ten years earlier and that five thousand pounds then might be worth seven or eight thousand pounds now. My lovely mother was convinced she was being fair and we were too excited to let the difference niggle.

Manney was delighted and did all he could to settle us into the business. He introduced us to the other market traders, including the man opposite who only sold bacon, and to all his suppliers. Everyone was so welcoming. We took on all Manney's stock and his staff, one of whom, Millie, became like a second mother to me. She was a wonderful little woman, even shorter than me, and she could sell anything to anybody; Millie was amazing.

On my first day my feet didn't touch the ground. We had to hang stock outside on rails and display nearly everything we had because there was nowhere to store anything. It was a completely different world and we were so busy. During the first week, every single day, Harold's face would appear at the back of the crowd. It was *typical* of Harold; he wanted to check I was all right. At the end of that first week I had to come clean. 'I want to be very truthful Harold, I can't manage on my own. It's just too busy.'

I didn't need to say anything else. Harold handed in his notice and came to join me. At that stage I was living at home with my mother in St John's Wood and Harold was living with his family in Wembley. I had my own car and Harold bought a van. On Wednesdays, which was half-day closing, we would go together to buy stock and then Harold would always come home to hand over fifty pounds to Mummy and have supper with us. Even after we got married we followed the same routine and we never missed one repayment until the loan was repaid in full.

If you look up the weather report for November 1961 you will read that it was a 'rather dry and sunny month with below average temperatures'. For 'below average temperatures' read 'freezing'. Uncle Jock was right; I had never, ever been so cold in all my life. For the first couple of weeks I insisted on wearing smart shoes and boots and Harold would rub my feet for me at the end of the day to try to get the circulation going again. Then I saw sense. The moment I bought a pair of fur-lined boots my world improved immediately. It was also obvious that there were advantages to the weather.

There were a lot of Jamaicans in Brixton in the early 1960s and if *I* thought it was cold, they thought it was like Antarctica. The colder it got, the more layers they bought. It was amazing for business. I have no idea how many hundreds of candlewick dressing gowns we sold: a wide range of colours and only 19s 11d (99p)!

By the time we got married in March 1962 we had been running the business for five months, so I knew Harold had a brilliant business head, was excellent at maths and always knew what to do. He also had an impressive work ethic and never once complained about being tired. We made a very good team. Harold was the sensible one and I would have the mad ideas. How perfect is that?

We had decided that we needed to live closer to work once we were married and Manney suggested we consider

Streatham. I had never even heard of Streatham, but we looked, and managed to get a three-bedroom flat in the same block as Manney, Leigham Hall on Streatham High Road. If you had to live in south London it was a prestigious block and even had a swimming pool. The pool was horrible really but we thought it was all grand, which is just as well as it cost the huge sum of twelve pounds a week in rent.

We had the most wonderful wedding. Mummy said she didn't think she had the energy to organise it but said Harold and I could have whatever we wanted and she would pay. I really lived a charmed life because when it came to anything my parents always had the best – the very best. There was a dressmaker in Bruton Street called Muriel Martin who had made my sister Helen's wedding dress and because she was still the best she made mine too. It was absolutely gorgeous: silk satin embroidered with lily of the valley, which is my favourite flower, and I also had lily of the valley in my bouquet. My two young nieces, Helen's daughters, Linda and Anne, were my bridesmaids and Muriel Martin made them the prettiest little dresses as well.

Mummy insisted that no expense was to be spared so I took her at her word and hired the very popular Sid Phillip's Big Band which is what I really wanted. Harold and I were married at St John's Wood synagogue and the reception was at the Café Royal in Regent St. It was all perfect until the time came for us to leave.

The plan was that I would change into my going-away outfit at the Café Royal and Harold's best man and best friend, David, would take my wedding dress back to Mummy's house. We had the suitcases for our honeymoon, but the bag I had packed with my going-away outfit was still in St John's Wood. I had no option but to leave the reception as I was.

In those days no one liked to admit they were newly-weds but walking through the lobby of the Piccadilly Hotel in my wedding dress was a bit of a giveaway. David had come with us as he still had to take my dress back to Mummy's, so the three of us went up to the room Harold had booked. Then there was a whole performance of how I was going to get my dress off and give it to David.

It seems funny now but at the time it was extremely stressful. Apart from my days at boarding school, I had never undressed in front of anyone. To make matters worse my nightie was in the same bag as my going-away outfit which meant that too was still in St John's Wood. The bedroom was pretty enough and while, thank God, there was a bathroom, we discovered that five pounds a night at the Piccadilly Hotel did not buy you windows. The room was ridiculously hot and because I was so nervous it got even hotter. Harold unzipped me and I went into the bathroom, wriggled out of my dress and bundled it round the door.

Unlike young people today, Harold and I had never slept together. It was really like marrying a stranger. It was all so new and intimidating. And then the next day you pretend you've been married for ages. I felt different but I was very keen that when we went on honeymoon no one would realise we had just got married. I just wanted to blend in. We went to Majorca which was lovely and I put up a good pretence of having been married forever but really I didn't know what day of the week it was.

The minute we got back from our honeymoon we moved into our new home in Streatham and I worked like crazy to get everything sorted. I am very fussy (plates are nearly clean before they go into my dishwasher) and in those days I was even more pernickety, but I organised everything in record time. No sooner had I got everything exactly as I wanted it than Harold threw me into a complete fluster. His family was more 'frum' than mine and he was used to following Jewish ritual more strictly than we did. Our wedding was on 18 March and 'Pesach' or Passover, the major spring festival, began that year exactly one month later. Harold insisted that we had to do it properly.

Jewish law dictates that all the pots, crockery and kitchen utensils that are used throughout the year may not be used on Passover (it's a long story) so I had to go out and buy new china and all sorts of things knowing that eight days later I would have to swap everything back again. No matter that we had hardly used what we had, I did what Harold wanted. I was determined to be the perfect wife.

Then I thought I would do a little more. Several years earlier my father had bought me a copy of *Jewish Cookery* by Florence Greenberg, the Jewish Delia Smith of her day. Mummy was a brilliant cook and I think Daddy thought that with the right book I could be too. A few days before Passover, I reached for Florence and looked up the recipes for cinnamon balls, coconut pyramids and macaroons. 'My Harold's going to be so impressed,' I told the shopkeeper when I went to buy all the necessary ingredients.

I got home and followed the recipes slavishly. The kitchen smelled wonderful but I ended up taking out of the oven one enormous cinnamon ball, one large lumpy macaroon and one congealed coconut pyramid range. Everything had merged. It was a complete disaster. I rang my mother in tears.

'The mixtures can't have been stiff enough,' she said. 'I don't understand how you didn't realise. How could you not have noticed?'

Of course I hadn't noticed. I had followed the recipes to the letter and thought that would do. Florence Greenberg would have ended up in the bin had my father not written a lovely inscription to his dear 'coch-lefel' inside the front cover. And Mummy set to baking and saved the day.

Once Passover was over I went to bed and couldn't get up. On top of organising the wedding, working in the shop, and setting up home, Passover proved to be too much. I was absolutely exhausted.

We hadn't been in Streatham long enough to have registered with a doctor but Harold was so worried he decided to ask the woman upstairs if she had any ideas. We didn't know the woman's name but as she used to scream 'Gates!' when anyone came in or out of the lift (because if the gates on the lift were not closed it couldn't go up to her floor), that is what we called her. Fortunately, Gates did know someone and a woman doctor came to see me. She was very brusque but positive and suggested the reason I was so tired might be that I was pregnant. She ordered me to stay in bed until I felt strong enough to get up and off she went.

Harold and I both wanted children and the idea that I might have fallen pregnant so quickly was wonderful. So we were bitterly disappointed when she was proved wrong. A year later she was still wrong and I went to see a gynaecologist who had been recommended by a friend. He said he would check me over to ensure everything was all right, but when I suggested it might have something to do with Harold rather than me, he corrected me. 'It is never the man,' he said. I must have looked amazed because to make sure I understood he repeated himself: 'It is never the man.'

In our case, that gynaecologist was proved wrong too.

Harold and I were distraught when the test results came back as we both desperately wanted a family. I decided to go and tell my mother as she was the most sensible person I have ever met and I was absolutely heartbroken. Mummy did not mince her words. 'You have two choices, June. You either adopt or you divorce Harold.'

'Divorce Harold?' I couldn't believe what she was saying as by that stage she loved Harold more than she loved me.

'I'm sure infertility is grounds for divorce,' she said.

I do not know if my mother was right or wrong but she was clever, because the shock of merely hearing the word 'divorce' was enough. I went home and began writing letters to every adoption society I could find.

We soon realised it was not as straightforward as we thought. We only wanted to adopt a Jewish child and everyone told us that Jewish babies rarely come up for adoption. The agencies said they would notify us if the situation changed but told us not to hold out any hope. We wiped away the tears and settled down to the matter of building up our business.

Brixton today is a very trendy place but in the 1960s it was a solid working-class area with the largest Afro-Caribbean community in the country. It was bursting at the seams, particularly with Jamaicans, whose culture and tastes jazzed up the dull London streets. Their food stalls were a real education; you could buy the most amazing things. Vegetables I had never seen before, let alone knew how to cook. Okra? Plaintains? Yams? Please!

What we did love was the buzz of the place – it was always busy and bustling.

Our shop was in the middle of Market Row, one of the three buildings that had sprung up during the 1920s and 1930s to form Brixton Market. Market Row was not, as it sounds, a straight line, but more of a T-shaped complex with market stalls below and offices above. It was sandwiched between Electric Avenue to the north, Atlantic Road to the east, Coldharbour Lane to the south and Electric Lane to the west. And there were three entrances, which meant customers could reach us every which way. It was a brilliant location and we didn't stop from the moment we rolled up the shutters until the time we hauled them back down again. We worked hard and we saved hard. Saturday was always our best day.

There are all sorts of rules about what you should and should not do on 'Shabbat', the traditional Jewish day of rest. It officially begins a few minutes before sunset on Friday night and lasts until three stars appear in the sky on Saturday night. We always observed (and still do) the Friday night rituals with family or very close friends. We make all the necessary blessings, light the candles, have 'challah', wine and dinner but, when we were business people, we always got up the next morning and went to work. Needs must.

We were doing brilliantly, and in 1964 we thought maybe we could do brilliantly somewhere else as well. Harold did the research and decided that Croydon had a lively market scene, so off we went to check it out. Surrey Street is the main market thoroughfare and we came across a wallpaper shop that wanted to sub-let one of its two units. After a little negotiation we took it, and our second Manney's opened at 18 Surrey Street, Croydon, that spring. We kept the name for various business reasons and we sold exactly the same stock as we did in Brixton: market trade is market trade after all. The big difference was that the Croydon shop had a proper front door and windows. I used to think of it as our 'grown-up' shop.

Once again, we were lucky in finding good staff. We have always employed people who want to work with us and even today, if we see anyone who has worked with us, they throw their arms around us and give us a lovely greeting. It is amazing, but I think it's because we never treated anyone differently; we were all, always, on the same team.

Harold and I shared out our time depending on where we were needed, but we still went buying on Wednesday afternoons because Wednesday was half-day closing in Croydon too. And we still went to have supper with my mother when we had finished.

Busy as we were, I never totally gave up the idea that we might, one day, become a proper family. Then we were told about an agency in Knightsbridge that looked after that rare creature – the Jewish baby who is put up for adoption. We filled in a huge number of forms, provided umpteen references and, eventually, we were invited for an interview with the National Children Adoption Association.

It was a nerve-racking experience but our names were added to their list. It was August 1965. We were told not to expect miracles but I was advised, just in case, to attend baby-care classes although, 'you must understand that it might be a total waste of time'.

It was very strange and quite difficult turning up to a hall full of expectant women when it was obvious that I was bump-free, but I was determined to put on a brave face. My friends and family had long since stopped telling me when mutual friends and acquaintances fell pregnant. Every woman of my age was expecting a baby, or so it seemed to me, but I had trained myself to be thrilled for them and to hide my own sadness.

The classes turned out to be far more fun than I expected and I could not wait until it was my turn to practise bathing 'baby': this was a privilege reserved for the women whose labour was just around the corner.

Three months later, completely out of the blue, we received a letter telling us that the agency had a lovely little boy for us and yes, he was Jewish. They invited us to their offices to meet David the following week, Thursday 2 December, 'when you will be able to take him home with you, if you like him'. If I liked him! I have never got over that expression. What natural mother has that option – and who could imagine that anyone would turn down such a wonderful and wondrous gift? The letter asked us to ring to confirm arrangements.

I was in the shop in Brixton when I made the call. 'Yes, yes, of course we will be there,' I said. It was impossible to hide my excitement.

'That's good,' said the woman on the other end of the phone. 'But you do know there is something wrong with the baby, don't you?'

'What?' Of course I didn't know. How could I have known? 'What's wrong with him?'

'He has talipes.'

I had no idea what that was, but it sounded so awful that I immediately dropped the phone and burst into tears. Harold calmly picked up the receiver and said we would call back.

Through my tears, I stammered an explanation of what the woman had said and Harold immediately picked up the phone again. He rang my brother-in-law, Helen's husband Melvin, who was a doctor, to ask what in God's name talipes was.

Melvin explained that talipes, or more correctly congenital talipes equinovarus, is the medical term for a club foot. It is when a baby's foot points downwards and inwards and the sole of the foot faces backwards. It was, Melvin said, quite common (we later learned that about one in a thousand babies in the UK is born with a club foot), it could be corrected and was not serious. 'Don't worry,' he said.

Don't worry! I could not stop crying. Off I went to see my mother.

Mummy (who grew not to just love David but to wor-ship him) advised me not to go ahead. She thought I was far too emotional to deal with such a problem. But I knew we had to go ahead. Had we been able to have a child naturally, we might have had a child with a club foot. I would have loved that baby without question and I would love this one in exactly the same way.

The next night I dried my tears and went to my baby-care class. I asked if I could have a go at the bathing business because, 'I'm having a little boy in five days' time'. It sounds absurd now but that was all the warning we had. Everyone was so happy for me and I went home feeling fairly confident that I could manage. Then we went out and bought everything you need for a new baby. Everything, in one swoop.

The following Thursday Harold and I went up to Knightsbridge as arranged. I don't think either of us had ever been so nervous and so excited all at the same time. In those days, babies were usually about six weeks old when they were given to their new parents, but David was three months old and had been with a foster mother since his birth. That kind woman handed me the most beautiful baby I have ever seen, no matter that he had a heavy plaster cast on his left foot. (God may have had a bit of trouble with one of David's feet but He did make him extraordinarily handsome.)

David's foster mother had been taking him to the hospital every week to have the cast changed, but that afternoon we had an appointment with an orthopaedic surgeon from Great Ormond Street Hospital to assess what we could do for our new little boy.

Mr Lloyd Roberts specialised in children's orthopaedics and was the most wonderful, wonderful man. He cut off the heavy cast, completely ignoring the loudest screams I have ever heard come from a small baby. He carefully examined David's foot and then invited us to sit down.

'First of all,' he said, 'don't worry. David will walk, he will play football, he will play cricket. In fact, he'll do everything a boy needs to do. I will make sure of that.'

George Lloyd Roberts was true to his word and continued to look after David until there was no more to be done. He never once let us down.

Many years later, when David was about twenty-one, we heard that Mr Lloyd Roberts had died. My gorgeous son was very upset at the news. There are not many people who genuinely change your life: that amazing man transformed David's completely. In turn, David transformed ours beyond my wildest dreams.

CHAPTER TWO

When you become a parent, inevitably you reflect on your own childhood. I remember mine as being wonderful, even though some of my earliest memories are of lying in bed, terrified that the Germans were coming to get us.

I had been born, like my two older brothers and sister, above my parents' shop in Kilburn High Road, but when war broke out we, and most of our extended family, moved to the relative safety of the 'countryside'. My father rented a large house in Newbury and one of his sisters, Fanny Matilda (always known as Fay) and her family, rented the one that backed directly onto it with an adjoining garden.

My oldest brother, Lewis, had already been called up and was serving in the Royal Corps of Signals and my other siblings, Gerald and Helen, went to whichever Newbury Grammar school was relevant to their gender. There were only sixteen months between Gerald and Helen, but it was a further nine years before I came along.

There is no glossing over the fact – I was a mistake.

The gap between Helen and me was such that my mother dismissed the idea that she could be pregnant. So, indeed, did her doctor. When Mummy reported feeling unwell, he sent her off to Czechoslovakia to 'take the waters'. It was only when she returned home suffering from hay fever and feeling worse than when she went, that the good man finally came to the conclusion that she was pregnant.

My arrival a few months later confirmed his diagnosis. I, June, was born in December – Saturday 7 December 1935 to be exact.

Less than four years later we were at war.

Once we were settled in Newbury, all the adults would go up to London on the seven o'clock train every morning while my cousin and I were left with one of a succession of nannies. Aunty Fay and Uncle Harry had three boys, the youngest of whom was only nine months younger than me and I adored him. Alan and I didn't do anything that we didn't do together.

One of our favourite adventures was riding our bikes. My parents were very good to us but they were not great present-givers so I never expected lavish gifts. Then came my seventh birthday. Alan already had a bike (a hand-me-down from one of his brothers I think) and my father obviously decided that I should have one too. The problem was that, during the war, it was impossibly difficult to buy children's bicycles – any spare steel went to the war effort – but Daddy bribed someone at Selfridges (with nylons I suspect) to sell him one. He then wheeled it all the way to Paddington Station, brought it home on the train and hid it until 7 December 1942. I will never, ever forget Daddy wheeling that bicycle into my bedroom on the morning of my birthday. It was the most memorable and most amazing present I have ever had. So many children do not realise how special some presents are, but for me that bike was the most special thing ever. Then, of course, I had to learn to ride it. The minute I got on I fell off. I did not want to admit to my father I was struggling so whenever he asked how I was getting on, I would just say, 'Well, I know how to stop.' Eventually, with Alan's help, I mastered it and we were off. We went everywhere on our bikes and I can honestly say that, apart from my unfounded dread about the Germans, Alan and I had a terrific war.

I was nine years old when peace was declared and my father decided it was safe to move back to London. During the war he had bought a beautiful house for 'frumpence' in Brondesbury Park, Willesden, and everyone was very excited at the prospect of moving into our own new home. Everyone, that is, except me.

I have no idea where the idea sprung from, but I decided that I definitely did not want to go to school in London. I wanted to go to boarding school so I could learn to ride. I adored horses from the moment my mother sat me on one on the Margate seafront when I was two years old.

'Going to the seaside' was a family ritual. My mother would rent a house in Broadstairs or Margate for the summer and install me, my siblings, her stepmother – known to us as Grandma Schneider – and a nanny. Daddy would stay in London and Mummy would travel up to help in the shop during the week and return to us at the weekends. Luckily for me, there was one occasion when she altered her routine and returned earlier in the week. It was on the very day that Nanny and Granny Schneider had left me for a while to my own devices. I must have been about three and, like all young children, I was rather fond of chocolate. I found a bar while I was rummaging through a cupboard, promptly ripped off the wrapper and devoured the whole thing. (I could not read, and even if I could have done, I doubt if I would have known what 'Ex-Lax' meant!)

I was so ill, but as Nanny and Granny Schneider did not know what to do, they did nothing. They even debated, I believe, not telling my mother. As it happened, Mummy did not need to be told that her curious toddler had consumed an entire bar of laxative chocolate. She knew the moment she saw me that I was in danger and whisked me off to hospital. Had she not acted so promptly, the doctors said, I might have died. I have no idea what my mother said to Granny Schneider and Nanny but I can imagine. What I do know is that I was never, ever left alone again.

The war put paid to our seaside adventures which did not upset me unduly, except that I lost the opportunity those holidays provided to climb (or more accurately, be plonked) on a horse.

Once the war was over I was desperate to stay in the country and learn to ride properly once and for all. I was only nine years old but city life did not fit my agenda. I now realise how amazing it was that Mummy and Daddy agreed.

My parents knew absolutely nothing about boarding schools, but off they went to have a look. They thought Kent might be nice, and not too far from London, so their first port of call was Benenden, which had been founded as a new public girls' school in 1923. Mummy felt the beds and decided they were too hard for her little princess. She then asked who looked after the girls' 'welfare'. Anyone who was Jewish would know that Mummy was really asking about food, but the headmistress was not Jewish. She assured my mother that she took care of the girls' academic progress and their welfare. Benenden was struck off the list.

Next up was Lillesden Girls' School, five miles down the road in Hawkhurst. The beds were also rather too hard for Mummy's liking but the welfare question was answered more to her satisfaction. The headmistress, Miss Mowatt, explained that she was in charge of the academic side of the school and that Miss Ireland took care of the girls' welfare. I was enrolled to start the very next term.

I was incredibly excited about the whole adventure but underestimated how overwhelming it would be. I had never been away from home. No sooner had I arrived at Lillesden than I started to cry. I was desperately homesick. I cried so much that in the end Miss Mowatt called my parents down to the school.

'You don't have to do this, June,' my father said. 'There are plenty of schools in London, you know.'

'We don't like seeing you so unhappy,' said Miss Ireland.

'Come home, darling,' my mother said.

'I'm staying,' said I.

And stay I did, for seven years.

Lillesden proved to be the most wonderful experience and was my first introduction to non-Jewish life. There were only four Jewish girls in the school but no one made us feel different. We went to prayers twice a day but we did not have to go to church on Sundays. We never came across even a pinch of anti-Semitism and I learned to get on with everyone, even the girls I did not particularly like. It was an amazing grounding and I am convinced that boarding school played a huge part in making me the person I am today. It is certainly where I first learned about dealing with money.

Every Lillesden girl had her own cheque book and her own paying-in book, and had to keep a personal accounts log. We paid our pocket money into the school 'bank' and when we wanted anything – no matter how small – we had to write a cheque to pay for it. One of the first cheques we all had to write at the start of every term was for the princely sum of three pence to cover 'Maids, Missions and Libraries' ('missions' being whichever charities the school was supporting that year). Our accounts books had to be kept up to date and were checked regularly so we could be allocated marks for accuracy and neatness. It was a fantastic system and a wonderful way to learn how to live within a budget.

Lillesden also allowed me to fulfil my dream of learning to ride. My very first term, I was enrolled at the nearby Benenden Riding Establishment – a very posh riding school run by Cherry Kendall (later to become Cherry Hatton-Hall) on her parents' farm. I was one of the first pupils to enrol after the war and many years later Princess Anne followed in my footsteps, as she too attended the Benenden Riding Establishment and was trained by Mrs Hatton-Hall. We used to have the opportunity to ride various horses but one of my favourites was a lovely pony called Gnome. She and I became very good friends indeed and I have many happy memories of riding Gnome.

I also loved sport (in truth, I was only interested in sport) but the most educational sessions, in terms of life skills, were mealtimes. Conversation during meals was obligatory. You had a different table each week and moved around the dining room. At the head of each table was a mistress or a sixth-former and you had to make conversation with them, as well as the person either side of you. We were not allowed to ask for anything, so everyone had to make sure that everyone else had what they wanted. It was an invaluable lesson for life. I also learned to make conversation with everybody and anybody. Again, how perfect is that!

It was while I was at Lillesden that I got my first bra. It was a Kestos bra, the first commercially produced bra to have two distinct and defined cups. Mine had cotton cups, ribbon straps and an elasticised strap at the back which crossed over and came round to the front to do up with a button under each cup. The school laundry was not versed in washing 'delicates' so usually, at the end of every term, all I would take home of my underwear was the name tapes. It was nothing if not very useful that my parents sold Kestos bras, so I always had a ready supply.

When I was about twelve years old my father had his first heart attack. (Collier men do not have strong hearts. My grandfather died before I was born and my brother Lewis was to die from a heart attack when he was only fifty-seven.) By this stage my parents had taken on two more women's wear shops – one in Chapel Street in Kilburn and one in Clapham. When Daddy fell ill, he sold off the two newer shops, as well as the lovely house in Brondesbury Park.

The doctor had ordered my father to rest every afternoon and Mummy decided that the easiest way to ensure that happened was to move back to live above the shop in Kilburn High Road. She did not care where she lived; her primary concerns were my father and the business.

The move back to Kilburn finally put paid to any thought that I might have had about bringing my schoolfriends home. I had made several good friends at Lillesden and had been to stay with one or two of the girls during the holidays, but I had always been nervous about returning the favour. I could not imagine how they would deal with chopped liver or egg and onion or any number of other things that were commonplace to me but which, I thought, would be very, very strange to them.

My friends were not especially wealthy but, to me, their homes were like mansions. We were not poor and probably even wealthier than several of my friends' families, but no other Lillesden girl lived above a shop. It was the first time I became aware that I was different. It was, I told myself, not a question of what I was, but merely where I lived. In the meantime, I set out to make the most of all Lillesden had to offer.

It was quite a small school, around a hundred and fifty pupils, and it was beautifully run. The one problem that developed, as we did, was the lack of male contact. The only men we ever saw were the man who cleaned the shoes and the doctor – and I was the picture of health.

During my last couple of years we were allowed to go out walking on a Saturday afternoon. Such heady freedom! We had to go in groups of four and to list our names in a special register. Each of us was allowed to cash a cheque for sixpence pocket money. Often we would combine our riches to buy a loaf of bread and a pot of jam. We would find a field and sit and eat our feast as if it were caviar. It was fantastic fun and it made me appreciate how lavish the food was that we enjoyed at home. (Food is very important in a Jewish household.)

I have kept all of my school reports from Lillesden and they are full of comments along the lines of, 'June is kind and sympathetic…' or 'June has become a very helpful member of the house…' Unfortunately, the remarks about my schoolwork do not make such happy reading.

It was generally agreed that it would be a miracle if I passed my O-levels and my father gave notice that I would leave school when I turned sixteen. I was not academic, so what was the point in my staying on at school? I understood his reasoning, but I was devastated because I loved Lillesden and wanted to continue.

And then, the miracle happened.

I was already back at home working in my father's shop when my results came through. To everyone's surprise, not least mine, I had passed all my O-levels, with the exception of art. But, sadly, it was too late to return to Lillesden.

There had never been any question that I would go into the shop. When Helen finished school she took her place behind the counter and I always knew that was expected of me too. I think that because our business was women's clothing, the boys had been given a freer rein. Lewis worked for a cinema chain and my father bought Gerald, who was mad about cars, a garage in Nether Street in Finchley.

Inspired and encouraged by my exam success, I gathered up enough courage to suggest I might like to train as a nurse. My mother stared at me as if I had gone mad.

'No, darling, you can't be a nurse,' she said, shaking her head. 'We're retailers. And besides, you'll never find anyone to marry you if you're a nurse. Nurses never get married.'

It was ridiculous, but she did not know what else to say to put me off the idea. Marriage, as far as Mummy was concerned, was a girl's main objective. I did not even dare to mention my secret and cherished ambition – to become a mounted police woman – as I suspected that would give Mummy heart failure.

I joined Helen behind the shop counter. I enjoyed selling and loved the lingerie so I was particularly pleased when my parents decided that I should learn to be a proper corsetry fitter. They sent me off to do an intensive course at the Berlei Corset School in Oxford Street. I loved it. We had lectures about women's anatomy and were taught how to fit the different bras (underwire was something of a novelty back then) and how to fit the different styles of corset that were available. (In those days some of the corsets did up at the side and were like long-line suspender belts that hooked up onto the bra band.) I really enjoyed the course, passed the exam with flying colours and went back to Kilburn with a new bounce in my step.

A year later, Helen married an army doctor. Melvin was the Regimental Medical Officer for the Horse Guards and we used to tease him endlessly about having to get the men to lie down before he could examine them, as the Guards were famous for being tall and Melvin is not. They had a lovely wedding and went off to live in a house that my parents bought and furnished for them.

Helen's marriage left me at home alone with my parents but I soon had a means of escape. My brother, Gerald, had started a driving school alongside his garage business and Mummy decided that Gerald had to teach me how to drive. Neither she nor my father drove and she came to the conclusion that it was important that I did.

I started lessons in the January and by the March I had passed my test. Daddy, of course, bought me a car. It was a Standard 10, which was one of the most popular small, four-door saloons of the day. Mine was painted a horrible grey, but I thought it was the most gorgeous thing I had ever owned.

Looking back on it, life was quite lonely in those days. My lovely cousin Alan was still a good friend during the holidays (he stayed on at school and then went up to Cambridge where he got a double first in History and English) but I did not know many people in London outside of the family.

My great joy was riding and I used to go to Hyde Park whenever I could. Then, one Sunday, I had an accident. I don't remember anything about the actual event, but apparently a dog ran out onto Rotten Row, my horse shied, I fell off and the horse kicked my head open, which it managed to do as my hat had fallen off.

The first thing I do remember is waking up in St George's Hospital with Gerald and my mother standing by my bed. When they left a nurse appeared at my side.

'I have to ask something,' she said. 'When I was helping to stitch you up you told me that I would never get married. Why? What made you say that?' The poor girl was obviously rather upset. I could not tell her that I had simply repeated what my mother had said, so I told her that I must have been delirious. I'm not sure that the poor nurse believed me, but what else could I say?

A week later, and still a little worse for wear, I returned home and to work.

Life carried on much the same as before. I made a few friends through the synagogue and we used to go to dances on Saturday nights, but I never enjoyed anything that came close to being a 'social whirl'.

Eventually, my father started to think about retirement and when Sainsbury's offered to buy his premises, he decided it was the perfect opportunity. He bought a lovely house in St John's Wood, signed the papers for the Kilburn sale and, for a moment or two, everything looked rosy.

The one glitch was that my mother had been suffering from terrible headaches for a while. When they got so bad that she could not get out of bed, the doctor sent her for a scan. The scan revealed that my mother had a brain tumour.

On 9 November 1958 – my father's sixty-fourth birthday – Mummy went into theatre at the Queen's Square Hospital.

After several anxious hours the surgeon came to see my father and told him that the operation had been very successful and the tumour was benign. 'Just give your wife a year and she'll be a new woman. Twenty years younger.'

'In that case,' joked my father, 'what can you do for me?' He had absolutely no inkling of what lay around the corner.

We had not yet moved, so Mummy came back to Kilburn and I took charge of looking after her. Everything was going well when, on 2 January 1959, my father was suddenly rushed to hospital with heart problems. He died the next day.

It was the most terrible shock. I adored my father but I had to be strong for Mummy's sake. There was no time for me to grieve; there were things that had to be done. At twenty-three years old I took on the responsibility for closing down the business and moving my mother and myself into the new house in St John's Wood.

My lovely Uncle Jock was a great support and sent people to help as much as they could, but it was a horrible, anxious time for me: a time that, thirteen years later, would come back to kick me sideways.

Mummy and I moved out of Kilburn in the February and I concentrated on helping her recover and settle into our new home. One day, one of Daddy's old suppliers, Phil Lee, rang to see how Mummy was recovering.

'And you, June? What are you up to?' Phil asked.

When I admitted that I was spending too much time just sitting out in the garden, he suggested, as a joke, that I could go to work for him. I nearly bit his hand off. I'm sure that he thought a boarding school princess from St John's Wood would last five minutes, but he offered me ten pounds a week and told me to start on Monday.

Phil's company, Victor Bright Ltd, was just what I needed. It got me out of the house and while I didn't make any real friends at work (only Phil and his brothers were Jewish) it was a busy place to be and I loved it.

Then one weekend I went to a dance and met a man called Arnold Eker. I was warned that he eyed up everyone in the book but I took no notice. I absolutely adored him.

Arnold was in the fabric business and worked just around the corner from me in Fitzrovia. It was all perfect.

Arnold proposed after we had being going out together for about a year. I was so excited that I put an announcement in *The Jewish Chronicle* before I even had a ring on my finger. (*The Jewish Chronicle* is the oldest Jewish newspaper in Britain and everyone, but everyone, reads it.) I had never been happier.

The following week Arnold came to see me and laid out his vision for our future. 'Obviously you'll have this house and we can live here,' he said.' Your mother will have to move out.'

I could not believe my ears. My mother move out of her own home! And even if she did, why should I inherit it over my sister and two brothers? I have never been so shocked – even to this day.

It was Arnold's mother, I am sure, who put him up to it, but before the week was out there was another announcement in *The Jewish Chronicle*. 'Amendment: Arnold Eker and June Collier are no longer engaged to be married.'

Helen and Melvin took me away for the weekend but I was utterly devastated. It took me ages to get over Arnold.

A year later Harold came into my life.

We had been work colleagues for a few years at this stage, and while I knew he was a lovely man, I had never thought of Harold as husband material. One day there was a lot of chat in the warehouse about the hit musical of the day (don't ask, I can't remember!). I really wanted to go but I had been told it was impossible to get tickets. Harold seemed to think he could solve the problem.

'Would you like to come with me on Saturday?' he asked. It did not occur to me that he was asking me on a date, I just thought that he, like me, wanted to see the show.

The following morning Harold came in with a huge smile on his face. 'I've got the tickets you wanted. We're going in April,' he said.

'April? I thought we were going on Saturday?'

'No, on Saturday we're going to *The Caretaker*.'

In spite of my reservations, we did go to Pinter's so-called masterpiece. I thought it was the most deadly, most boring play I had ever seen, yet somehow I ended up going out with Harold again.

Many, many years later, at our Golden Wedding Anniversary party, Harold brought up the subject of our first date. 'June, have you ever thought that there might've been tickets available for the show you wanted to see that Saturday night?'

Of course I had never considered that. Why would I?

My gorgeous husband warmed to the theme. 'Have you ever thought that my strategy was, if I booked three months ahead, it'd give us a chance to get to know each other better?'

I do not know if Harold really was that devious, and I never will. For one very important reason that I will tell you about later, the answer will remain a mystery forever.

CHAPTER THREE

When we first set up shop in Croydon I thought I would go mad with the noise.

There was (and still is) a row of food stalls running the full length of Surrey Street between the shops. If that wasn't bad enough, the woman who had the pitch outside our shop used to broadcast her wares at the top of her voice. All day, every day, in competition with the other traders who took the same approach to attracting customers, she would cry out, 'Mushrooms!' as loudly as she could. It was nerve-racking.

'Mushy', as we called her, turned out to be very friendly and I eventually learned to ignore her screeching. She was just one of the people who were delighted for us when David came into our lives. There was a real sense of community in Surrey Street and everyone was so kind.

Surrey Street is meant to be the oldest street market in London and, while I can't swear that's true, I do know that there's been a market in Croydon since the thirteenth century. It has had an assortment of names over the years, most associated with meat – The Shambles, The Flesh Market, The Butcherie and Butchers' Row – but it's been Surrey Street for as long as anyone I know can remember.

From the minute we had David I had to step back from the business, both in Croydon and Brixton. Not only were there so many things to learn, but I also had to take him to Great Ormond Street Hospital three times a week to have his foot strapped. They had to straighten David's foot and lower his heel and Mr Lloyd Roberts thought that would be done best through constant strapping and re-strapping rather than with a plaster cast.

It was an anxious time in so many ways and, to make matters worse, there was a delay in the legal side of things. When you adopt a child, you have to go to court to have the adoption order signed by a judge; only then do you have full parental rights and responsibilities. Normally it takes between twelve and sixteen weeks, but we had to wait nine months. Mummy found it very stressful as she adored David, and I was a complete bundle of nerves. I loved him instantly and was terrified that we might lose him. He was so beautiful I used to tiptoe into his bedroom and stand over his cot when he was asleep just to watch him.

I couldn't believe he was ours and, at last, he was. We brought David home in the December 1965 and the following September his birth mother finally signed the last document and we went to court.

To commemorate the occasion my sister, Helen, gave us a lovely silver 'kiddush' cup, a wine goblet used on the Sabbath, on which she had had the court date engraved beneath the inscription, 'A Date to Remember'. The cup became my greatest treasure.

Life settled down to a busy routine. Harold was wonderful. He coped with everything and just took it all in his stride. While he bore the brunt of the business affairs, I helped whenever I could, especially with the buying. I just had a feeling for what would sell. I think you either have it or you haven't. There was a limited choice in those days but provided you had the right thing, in the right colour at the right price, it sold. It was fascinating really.

When our five-year lease on our flat in Streatham was coming to an end, we decided that we should think about buying our own home. We needed more room, if only to put in a washing machine and dryer to cope with all the nappies. (I was fed up with rinsing them out at home and then lugging them down to the local launderette.) It made sense to us to look at properties in Croydon.

The Whitgift estate, named after a rather flashy sixteenth-century Archbishop of Canterbury, looked just right. There were some lovely houses and, best of all, the estate backed onto woods and fields.

I found what I thought was the perfect house and was beside myself when I discovered it had already been sold. I confess I did make a bit of a fuss, but for years afterwards I used to drive past it and think, 'Thank God we didn't get that place.' (I admit that I'm one of those people who get fixed on an idea and sometimes have to accept later that I was wrong.)

The home we were to live in for the next thirty-five years was the reason for my change of heart: 23 Fitzjames Avenue was a mock Tudor house with a fantastic garden. No matter that the interior was horrific – it had been split up into bedsits for a group of Seventh Day Adventists and needed to be completely gutted.

There was another couple who wanted the property but what swung it in our favour was that we had David. The seller thought it would be nice for the house to go to a family with a little boy who would enjoy the swing in the garden.

The asking price was £11,000 and we only had £3,000 but we were determined. My mother was against the whole idea. As far as she was concerned it was too expensive and we were aiming 'above our station'. Please!

It did not help that we had trouble getting a mortgage because of the state of the place. But Harold did not give up. We did get a mortgage, even though it was a terrible one, and we set about making the house our home.

It was around the same time that we had a double blow in the family. Uncle Toby, married to my father's sister, Miriam, died on the very same day as Uncle Jock. I was fond of Uncle Toby but I adored Uncle Jock. Like all the Collier men, he had heart problems. He died when he was only sixty-eight, just a few months after he had donated £50,000 towards a new heart research centre at Hammersmith Hospital.

The newspapers were full of stories about 'the shy magnate with 1,000 shops' who had started out in business when he was still in his teens with £30 and a big ambition. (They did not know that he had also had a lot of help and guidance from my father.) Uncle Jock was very well known in his day because he had transformed the old Fifty-Shilling Tailors into John Collier, the chain with the famous 'Window to Watch' advertising slogan, and also included the United Drapery Stores in his huge empire. UDS was one of the biggest clothing retail groups in the country at the time and it has been claimed that, in 1966 alone, they sold more than a million men's suits.

What the papers did not go into was the fact that Joseph Collier's original family name was Coblenz. His parents had fled Russia at the end of the nineteenth century and made their way to Britain. (There are no exact numbers, but I have read that there was a huge wave of immigration between 1880 and 1905, when between 200,000 and 450,000 Russian Jews arrived in the UK.)

Uncle Jock's parents couldn't speak a word of English and when they were asked their name on arrival, obviously, completely misunderstood. For some reason they said 'Coblenz', which is a city in central Germany, and that immediately became their surname.

All through the First World War they were Coblenz; then in about 1920, the boys decided to change their name to Collier. I have no idea why they made the choice they did, but their mother, who was a widow by then, changed her name as well.

Harold's family also changed their name at around the same time, again because of the anti-German feeling after the first war. In their case, Kleinman became Kenton. It wasn't as if both decisions were without royal precedent: only three years before King George V had changed his family's name from Saxe-Coburg-Gotha to Windsor.

Uncle Jock had always been very good to us and when he died he left Helen and me £5,000 each, which is the equivalent of nearly £65,000 today. I don't know what Helen did with her windfall but quite a bit of mine went on doing up our new house.

Business continued to flourish and in 1969 we took on a third unit in Brixton and filled it with lingerie. It proved to be a very good decision and trade went from strength to strength.

We had also been back in contact with the National Children Adoption Association in Knightsbridge because we wanted another child. They were very happy at how well we had coped with David but they told us not to hold out any hope. 'So few Jewish children come up for adoption...' etc etc etc. We accepted the situation and concentrated on the lovely child we had.

David was four when the time came for his first operation on his foot. I went to the office in Great Ormond Street and explained that I was coming into hospital with him. The woman behind the desk was quite taken aback.

'You can't do that,' she said. 'Nobody comes in with their children.'

'I do. If David falls over and grazes a knee I pick him up and make it better. He can't have a major operation without me. It wouldn't be right. What happens if he cries?' I was not going to be put off.

'You can go all over the hospital and you won't find any child crying,' she said.

'Only because they're too frightened to cry,' I spat back.

During our first meeting with Mr Lloyd Roberts four years earlier he had asked if we wanted David to be treated privately or on the NHS. We had said we would do whatever was best for David. I will never forget Mr Lloyd Roberts's reply: 'I have a lot of wealthy patients who pay for my services, so go with the NHS. I promise I will look after David.'

I thought of that conversation as the hospital clerk explained that if I wanted to come into hospital with David we would have to go privately. That, of course, is what we did. And I am so glad we were in a position to be able to do so. At night you could hear the children crying and I didn't know which one to run to first!

Shortly after David and I got home, Harold came up with the idea of opening another shop, this time in the new shopping centre that had recently opened in Croydon. The first shop in the Whitgift Centre, Boots, had opened in 1968, and the centre itself was due to be officially opened in October 1970 by the Duchess of Kent, wife of the Queen's first cousin, Prince Edward.

Harold thought we should be in on it.

Yet again, my mother was not keen. 'You need to be on the High Street,' she insisted. 'Centres just don't work.' Mummy was a very good businesswoman and her advice was in keeping with the thinking of the time. The boom time for shopping centres was just around the corner, but in 1969 they were considered to be dead.

Harold and I talked about the idea a lot and decided that if we took a shop in the Whitgift Centre we would concentrate on lingerie and swimwear and offer proper fittings. I have no idea why we had that idea, but I think it was because my mother only ever wore made-to-measure and I thought that proper fittings would help women who could not afford such a luxury.

We decided to add swimwear to the range because you need as much fitting for a swimsuit as you do for a bra. Most women hate buying swimwear, but we thought that if you were being fitted for a bra, how wonderful would it be if someone helped you find a swimsuit that fitted as well. (It is so important that swimwear is fitted.)

Against my mother's advice, we leased a unit in the Whitgift Centre on the first floor. It was in a very good position en route from the car parks to Marks & Spencer and we thought it had great potential. It was so exciting but we struggled to think of a name for our new shop. It was going to be in a completely different league to either Manney's, so we wanted something appropriate and memorable. We asked everybody we knew and one night, when we were at a dinner party, some very good friends of ours, Freda and Lionel Ziman, suggested 'Contour'. We thought it was brilliant and Freda and Lionel were thrilled when we decided to use their idea.

Finally, everything was in place and we worked towards opening our first really posh shop in May 1970.

Then suddenly, on the personal front, there was a very exciting development.

In April, completely out of the blue, we received a letter from the adoption agency saying that they had a lovely little girl we could take home the following week, 'if you like her'. That stupid expression again! Like her? We fell in love with her instantly. She had beautiful blonde hair and huge brown eyes. She could have been mistaken for an angel. She was only six weeks old and we called her Jill because we wanted a straightforward and simple name.

As soon as I had Jill, I had to stay at home to look after her so, instead of me going out to buy the stock we needed for Contour, all the reps came to us. It was fantastic. Harold and I bought everything we needed for the new shop from our living room.

David had less than a week to get used to the idea of having a sister but he was wonderful with her from the moment she arrived. He knew he was adopted and he knew Jill was too. We always told the children from the very beginning that they were special because they were chosen. Not long after we had Jill, Harold took David to nursery where he informed all the other children that he and his sister were special. 'We're different from you because we were chosen,' he said. He was so convincing about how it was so much better to be chosen that several of the other children ended up in tears!

It was a wonderful time. I loved looking after the children and Harold took his new enlarged family commitments and business interests in his stride. The whole adoption process was also much quicker for Jill as her birth mother had already signed the necessary papers. We went to court at the first available opportunity.

To mark the occasion Helen gave us another beautiful silver kiddush cup engraved with the same inscription and the date. It was, indeed, another date to remember but, as we had the cups to remind us, I did not engrave either on my heart. How I wish that I had!

A few years later our home was burgled and all our silver was stolen, including my two precious silver cups. And yet, while now I cannot remember the exact dates, I will never forget the relief and joy of those two special days. The first when our beautiful little boy officially became our son, and the second, five years later, when our gorgeous little girl became our very own daughter.

How lucky and blessed were we?

One of the first things we had to do when we set up Contour was hire a window dresser. In Surrey Street we put examples of everything we had in the window, because that's how markets work, but in a shopping centre things are different. Our windows were still full of merchandise but it was more artfully displayed!

Again, we were very lucky with staff and it soon became obvious that we had hit on a brilliant idea. Contour was successful because people could see we were getting it right and they kept coming back. What is more, the centre was one of the first in the country to take off. People loved it.

I went in to the shop whenever I could and found that I often thought of my father. Daddy knew exactly what to buy for Kilburn – he was a genius at it – and turned his shop into a goldmine of a business. Almost every day he would walk up and down the High Street and see what everyone else had and their prices. He would never be more expensive than anyone else and, if he could, he would reduce the price. 'You must know what your customers want and you must offer them value, June,' he used to say. Harold and I followed his creed.

There was nothing like the choice of bras we have today, so what we did was fit the front and alter the back. We did not have our own workroom but we had brilliant outworkers who could keep up with the demand. And what a demand!

We were the first people to introduce size thirty bras because we were taking in so many thirty-twos (women were narrower in those days). We bought most of our stock from our normal suppliers but when it came to D and double D we had to buy from America. It seems absurd now, but back then, there was no one in the UK making bras with larger cups and we always had a waiting list.

We were also very fussy about training our staff. When someone started with us she did not fit a customer for three months; she merely observed the trained fitters. Then, when she did start fitting on her own, she would be checked for several more months until we were happy she was up to scratch.

We did everything – and still do – by eye. I am passionate about the benefits of a properly fitted bra and having learned about corsetry fitting initially when I was still in my teens, I took every opportunity afterwards to attend all the fitting schools that were offered by the major lingerie manufacturers. It was a revelation because it did not take me long to realise that relying on a tape measure to give you an accurate size just does not work. Numbers cannot tell you if a woman has a narrow back and everything at the front or, conversely, if she has a broad back and nothing at the front. You have to look and assess, and we became very good at it: fitting became our USP (unique selling point).

Harold was the money man and did all the office work but, if we were particularly busy, he would come out into the shop. There were days when we were so hectic that there might only be Harold and a junior on the shop floor. If a customer did not want to wait for a fitter, the junior would usher the woman into a fitting room and Harold would stand outside. Then the junior would come out and Harold would hand her a number of different of bras to take back in to the customer that he thought would fit. Invariably, he was right. Harold has never been in a fitting room in his life but he has always had a good eye.

One of our games, if we were stuck at traffic lights, would be to take it in turns to decide on the cup sizes of the women crossing the road. It always amazed me how often Harold and I agreed.

That isn't to say he did not sometimes get it wrong; one of David's favourite stories is about one of his dad's off days. David was in the shop with Harold when a customer came in looking for help. Harold explained that all the fitters were busy and asked the woman to wait. As soon as one of the girls was free he explained there was a lady who needed assistance before adding in a whisper, 'I think she's looking for a maternity bra.'

Unfortunately, Harold wasn't quiet enough. The woman spun round and looked him in the eye. 'I am not pregnant!' she snapped.

David says that he has never seen his father make such a quick exit.

I could not give as much time to the business as I would have liked because both Harold and I were of the same opinion – a mother should bring up her children – so we found a routine that worked for us. I have always had a daily woman to help me and my first came to work for us when we were living in the flat in Streatham. Her name was Agnes Crisp. Agnes was originally from Norfolk but when she was fourteen her mother had sent her to one of the big houses in Regents Park in London to learn the art of being 'in service'. It was one of those houses where all the grates had to be cleaned before the family got up so Agnes had to start work at six every morning. She must have been in her fifties when she came to us but her training stood her in good stead. Agnes was a woman who knew how to keep everything in order.

When David was learning to talk he could not say the word Agnes, so for some reason he decided to call her Hattie. It stuck, and from then on that is what we all called her. She used to have to walk goodness knows how far to get to us in Streatham but, when we moved to Croydon, Hattie came too. Her official working hours were from nine to three, so she would have lunch with us every day. As was common when Hattie was young, her mother bought her a typical wedding present at that time: she paid to have all of Hattie's teeth taken out so that her husband would not have to worry about paying for dentists in the years to come. Unfortunately, Hattie's dentures did not fit particularly well and every lunchtime we used to sit in the kitchen trying our best to ignore Hattie's clicking teeth.

We were all devoted to Hattie and she to us. She adored David and Jill to such an extent that she treated them like her children, even though she had two of her own. Hattie was with us for nineteen years and we were distraught when she decided to retire.

We also had a wonderful babysitter for years, Mrs Harmer, known to the children as Hamper, who for all the years she was with us drove a battered old Morris Minor. With the help of Hattie and Hamper I could keep up with what was going on in Croydon and Brixton, even if I could not spend a lot of time in the shops. It also helped that my mother adored the children.

At the end of the summer of 1971 Mummy had to have a hysterectomy and, to our horror, the doctors discovered that she had leukaemia. It was a terrible shock as there had been no indication at all that she was ill.

Three months later she was dead – and I fell apart.

When my father died there had been no time to grieve. I had to be strong for my mother and there was a lot to do to close the family business and move house. When Mummy died, I grieved for both her and my father. I grieved so much that I fell seriously ill.

The doctors diagnosed tuberculosis, although they had no idea how or why I might have contracted it, and I spent eleven weeks in the Brompton Hospital. It was very hard on Harold who had to deal with the children, our home and the business, but, as ever, he was amazing.

It took me a long time to recover but recover I did. I knew that the best thing I could do was to channel my energies into Harold, the children and our business. I knew that is what my parents would have wanted.

Contour in the Whitgift Centre went from strength to strength. We started going to the big trade shows in Dusseldorf, Lyons and Paris as well as on buying trips to Germany and Israel to visit the best swimwear companies in the world. Harold again knew what we wanted. He hated swimsuits that were lined in white and wherever we went the first thing the suppliers would say is, 'Don't worry, Harold, we have beige lining.' He was one of the very first retailers to appreciate that beige, or skin-coloured, lining is far more discreet.

We loved all our trips abroad but, for obvious reasons, we loved our buying trips to Israel the most. They were all the more special because one of Harold's younger brothers, Jack, lives there with his family, and the younger of his two children is the same age as David.

Harold was the second of four boys and his parents had a fish and chip shop on the Goswell Road in Islington. When Harold was growing up, his family, like mine, lived over the business until they could afford a house, in Willesden. I never had the opportunity to meet Harold's father, because he died from kidney failure when he was only forty-nine. Harvey, the eldest son, was twenty at the time and already working in the 'schmutters' business, but he took on the bulk of the responsibility for the family. Harold, at eighteen, had to do his national service and the two youngest, Jack and Gerry, were still at school.

When Harold returned from the Royal Air Force he worked first as a sales rep in women's clothing for a company called Dukes. He then joined Phil Lee at Victor Bright, one of the companies that supplied my parents' shop in Kilburn, which is, of course, where we met.

Jack went to Israel as soon as he finished school; and Gerry never really recovered from an accident he had when he was in his teens. (He was run over by a bus while riding his bike in Cricklewood. He lost a leg and, with it, all his confidence and motivation.) Harvey died a while back; Jack is still in Israel; but Gerry never married and continues to live a quiet life in Wales.

Jack ended up as an Israeli diplomat and we liked to visit him if we could, wherever he was posted. At one time he was Israeli ambassador in Cameroon and we spent a very memorable three weeks there; and on another occasion we went to see him when he was Israeli ambassador in Brazil. (Jack's wife, Tirtza, is Brazilian, so he was fluent in Portuguese long before they went there in an official capacity.)

Harold and I have always done everything together but, at work, we had our defined roles and our two worlds rarely collided. Harold couldn't go into a fitting room and I never thought about the money. We were just one.

We did so well that after a few years we decided that we should open another Contour, and we fancied trying our hand in central London. One day we were up at Harrods and while we were there we thought we would have a look around. We were just mooching really and had no intention of looking for premises. In those days the Hans Road side of Harrods was the 'blind' side – there was only one door that allowed public access to the shop. It was a very quiet street but near the Brompton Road end there was an old-fashioned shop called The Corset Boutique which caught our eye.

Harold and I went in and had a quick look around before going up to the elderly couple behind the counter. Never having been short of 'chutzpah', I decided to get straight to the point. 'Would you like to retire?' I asked.

'When?' they said, staring at me as if I was heaven-sent. 'When, when, when?'

It turned out they were dying to give up. It also turned out that they did not own the shop but merely ran it. (Bizarrely, the people who did own the shop, Mr and Mrs Rind, had another in Streatham High Road, right by the entrance to our old flat in Leigham Hall.)

The Corset Boutique was quite tatty and downstairs there was only a coal hole and an outside toilet. We knew it would a need a lot of work to turn it into a Contour but the big plus was that the rent was frumpence – a mere five hundred pounds a year.

It took a few months to do the deal and we had to send in the shop fitters before we could even think about opening the doors. We completely revamped the upstairs and converted the downstairs to accommodate a proper cloakroom, a work room and an office. ('Office' is a generous word for what was not much more than a glorified cupboard, but a lot of good things happened in there.)

We knew we would be able to sell more up-market items in Knightsbridge so we adapted and bought different stock for the different areas. There was no difference at all in physical size of the customer in Croydon and the customer in Knightsbridge – the difference was in the size of their purse.

We finally opened our second Contour in the middle of 1977 and I will never forget our first day. We had some very pretty nightwear sets with a ticket price of a hundred pounds. I thought it was ridiculous. 'They'll never sell, Harold. Who'd pay a hundred pounds for a nightie and negligee?'

I had my answer before lunch.

An Arab gentleman came in and, without a second thought, bought a set. I was so excited I had to ring absolutely everybody I knew. I could not believe it. I can still feel the elation now; it was such a huge sale for us.

Little did I know that it was a sign of things to come.

CHAPTER FOUR

For a Jewish boy, the 'bar mitzvah' is one of life's landmarks. It is a big deal.

David's thirteenth birthday was approaching in August 1978 and we had decided it was going to be a memorable occasion. We knew we wanted to have a man called Ivor Spencer as toastmaster which meant we needed to book him a long way in advance. Ivor was the founder chairman of the Guild of International Toastmasters and was, quite simply, the best. (By the time he retired, Ivor had been the Master of Ceremonies at more than a thousand royal occasions, as well as at countless other events.) Ivor was also very, very good at public relations.

The advertising budget for our business had always been infinitesimal because we discovered very early on that word of mouth is the best form of advertising, with the added bonus that it is free. But suddenly we had to establish Contour in Knightsbridge and also ensure that our Croydon Contour got the publicity it deserved. Normally that job would fall to me, but at the time I had a lot of other things that demanded my attention (I'll tell you later) so we decided that we needed help.

Ivor did the publicity for a company that sold hair restorer and we were reading about that every five minutes. If he can do that for hair restorer, we thought, imagine what he could do for us! We took a deep breath and asked Ivor for help. His fee for a year was an eye-watering five thousand pounds, but we wanted to learn and thought we should learn from the best.

Enter Ivor.

The first press release he circulated was about what Contour offered women who had had mastectomies – a subject close to my heart. With the advancement in diagnosis for breast cancer we were seeing more and more women who needed help. I thought the hospitals were getting it wrong and prided myself that we were getting it right.

It is a dreadful scenario. You have a mastectomy and suddenly, once you have lost a breast (or, God forbid, both breasts), you become a client of the Appliance Department. You are only two or three hours older after your operation and yet the mere mention of the 'Appliance Department' makes you feel as if you have aged beyond measure.

The next major problem comes when you are visited by someone from said department who asks what size bra you wear. Most women have not got a clue: 85 per cent of women wear the wrong size bra because they have never been properly fitted! So you say the size you think you are, which only makes things worse. I have seen scores of prostheses over the years that are the wrong size and do not fit properly.

Every hospital should tell their mastectomy patients to go and get a bra fitting before they supply them with a prosthesis. It's important to assess the good side and then try a range of prostheses, because every woman is different. It is also important, I think, that the fitting is done in a fashion context because you need to feel like the woman you are.

I can also tell you, from years of experience, that the fitting room is often the first place where a woman feels she can let her emotions show.

'How are you?' asks your doctor after your operation.

'I'm fine,' you lie.

And nine times out of ten you repeat that lie to your family because you don't want to upset them. You want them to believe that, now you've had your operation, everything is going to be rosy.

In a fitting room a woman does not have to be a stoical wife or mother, she can admit how awful the whole thing is and how miserable it makes her feel. I am sure it's the old thing about opening up to strangers, but over the years I have had a lot of women break down in the fitting room. I have always felt a huge responsibility to ensure that such a customer leaves me with a smile on her face.

I really believe that ours is the only branch of the retail business that changes lives. A new dress or a new pair of shoes can cheer you up, but a good, well-fitted bra is life-changing; never more so than when you have had a mastectomy.

The press release Ivor issued was very much along the same lines and it was reproduced in papers all over the country. I was thrilled, not just because of the mention of Contour, but because I was, and still am, passionate about the post-operative care of mastectomy patients. I think we got the coverage we did because I was speaking from the heart and what I was saying was, and, once again, still is, important.

The following month, I learned another valuable lesson. We were asked to contribute an item to the world's biggest jumble sale that was being held in Olympia as a fund-raiser for Save the Children. Thousands of people had sent bits and pieces including Margaret Thatcher, then Leader of the Opposition, who donated a silk headscarf. The actor, Peter Sellers, sent a pair of men's silk pyjamas (with a lipstick smear on the sleeve) and the former Prime Minister, Edward Heath, gave a velvet smoking jacket.

'Don't just send a swimsuit, June. Donate something that stands out,' said Ivor. 'Something outrageous to capture the photographers' attention.'

A pink mink bikini, I thought, would do the trick. And sure enough, once filled by the shapely model Kirstie Pooley, she, it, and Contour, made the front page of the *Daily Express* and the *Evening Standard*, and featured in most of the other papers as well.

It was a hectic year. Ivor came up with something every month. The popular television dance group, Second Generation, caused a stir in the Whitgift when they flitted around the centre modelling Contour swimwear and lingerie; and we used a similar trick to bring the traffic to a halt on the Brompton Road. 'A New Tourist Attraction', was the title of Ivor's press release.

CONTOUR, the exclusive Knightsbridge lingerie and swimwear store, will be putting on a fashion show with a difference from Friday 2nd June for one week at 11.00 a.m. for one hour.

Instead of their top models showing the styles inside the store, the girls will parade in the open in Knightsbridge wearing the latest mini-bikinis, swimwear and lingerie from the great fashion houses worldwide.

The reaction was fantastic. I thought we might have gone too far when I got the girls to lie down on the zebra crossing, but everyone loved it. Ivor had said we planned to repeat the show every year, but of course we did not do that. We would never have got the same coverage again – and we got a lot of coverage.

That particular stunt did highlight one small problem, mind you. The Knightsbridge models all carried Contour signs, but in the papers I was quoted simply as June Kenton – there was no immediate and obvious connection between me and Contour. I decided the thing to do was 'change' my name.

The next day I took down my certificates from all the top lingerie companies that were on display in the shop and sent them off to be altered. Within a week they were back on the walls, but with the name June Kenton changed to June Contour.

The next story that excited the press quoted June Contour talking about how Middle Eastern shoppers in London were setting new challenges. Ivor's story told of a Knightsbridge customer who wanted thirty bra and knickers sets for the ladies who were staying with him as his guests. The underwear sets had to be all the same design and the same colour but in a range of different sizes. According to Ivor, we met the demand and the grateful gentleman added more than £3,000 to our takings for the day.

In truth, some of our very best customers were from the Middle East. We had the most amazing nightwear and often someone would come in from one of the Middle Eastern royal families and choose a selection of different things. We would then take the chosen items to the Grosvenor House, or the Dorchester, or wherever they were staying. They always had suites so there was an ocean of space where they would put up rails for us to hang our stock. Sometimes we would have to wait hours and hours before we saw a soul. Eventually we realised that, usually, the women did not get up before about five o'clock in the afternoon. They then needed a few more hours before they were ready to come and choose what they wanted. It was madness really, but a very lucrative sort of madness. We rarely took anything home.

Ivor then told us that Wimbledon was considering advertising on the centre court. Harold immediately wrote a letter offering to pay £10,000 if we could have Contour hoardings up for the Ladies Final. He suggested the wording could be along the lines of, 'Contour of Knightsbridge, for the finest lingerie and swimwear'. The All England Club Secretary, Major David Mills, wrote a charming letter in response. Unfortunately he declined Harold's offer, but that, in itself, made another good story for the press.

Then Ivor excelled himself.

He rang me at home one night. 'I thought you should know,' he said, 'I've just sent out a press release saying that you think British boobs are best.'

'Why? I've never said that.' I was more than a little alarmed.

'You have now. So you'll just have to think up some answers for when they ask you why.'

I did not have much time. The phone went mad.

British boobs are well-formed and shapely. What is wrong with French boobs? A little small. Italian? Too much pasta, so quite full. German? A little too athletic. On and on it went. America, Australia and even Japan. It was amazing. The story went round the whole world.

It was a brilliant public relations exercise, not only because of the enormous coverage it gave to Contour, but also because it set me up as one of the leading and most knowledgeable 'boobologists' of the day (boobology being the only '-ology' I have).

And it was not only us who benefited from Ivor's imagination. Rex Features, one of the major London news agencies, won best agency of the year on the strength of how they used the campaign.

In the middle of all the wild stunts Ivor dreamed up, we had David's bar mitzvah and Ivor was, indeed, the Master of Ceremonies for what turned out to be a really wonderful party. We thought it would be something different to hire Woburn Abbey for the occasion. We organised coaches to take everyone to Bedfordshire from our house in Croydon and just after they had arrived I saw what I thought was a group of boy scouts walking down the middle of our road. 'Why, Harold? Today of all days? The boy scouts have never come down here before. They'll just get in the way!' I was furious.

Harold had to stop laughing before he could tell me to look again. He realised long before I did that my 'boy scouts' were a group of our friends dressed as if they were going on a real safari. It was the most wonderful prank and added enormously to what was an unforgettable day. We started with tea and then our guests could tour the safari park and/or the house before meeting up again for a formal dinner and a dance in the main ballroom.

As you might imagine, we all go to a lot of bar mitzvahs, but I think (biased though I am) that David's is remembered as something special. There is a wonderful photograph album of the event and I cherish a three-page poem that one of our guests sent as a thank-you letter. It is so clever because it includes every element of the day in perfect rhyme! It never fails to make me smile.

When our time with Ivor was coming to an end he told me to be prepared for the fact that Prince Charles would soon get engaged. 'It's imminent, June. Be ready.' Ivor was a past master at keeping up with the toings and froings of high society and used to send gifts to the royals at any and every opportunity. Every year he bought a bottle of champagne for the Queen Mother which he personally delivered to Clarence House on the 4 August – her birthday.

We did exactly as we were told. We bought a nightdress and peignoir set which we could send to the prospective Princess of Wales when the announcement came. 'Don't forget to take photographs of the set – preferably on a model,' Ivor said. 'Send out the photo and the story to the press the minute you dispatch the box to Kensington Palace.' Unfortunately, it turned out that Ivor's timing was seriously amiss.

When we realised there was not going to be an engagement announcement we wrapped up the gorgeous silkiness in tissue and put it in a safe place. We were 'ready' for when Prince Charles finally took the leap. As you will discover, the stunt did not go entirely to plan and could have been a very costly affair had it not been for Harold's cousin. But more of that later…

Working with Ivor had been a wonderful rollercoaster ride but when his contract ran out, I felt ready to take over. I had learned so much; not least that, to promote your company, you have to keep coming up with ideas and you must *always* send out a press release. Public relations companies use a formula, I believe, to work out the monetary value of editorial column inches (based, I assume, on the advertising rates for different papers and magazines) but I think editorial space is priceless. You pick up trade by people walking past your shop, but that is as nothing compared to how many people you reach through the press. If you are doing a good job, shout about it.

We were doing a good job: I shouted.

We had a lot of success in Croydon with 'Men Only' nights, which we usually held at Christmas, because that is when men go into panic mode. When we first started most of the men who came did not have a clue. We would all have to line up and they would say, 'A bit like you, but maybe a bit more like her'. It was ridiculous. And you knew that whatever they bought, it was coming back.

Me in my prime!

My parents: Harry Collier and Ray (Rachel) née Schneider, c. 1955.

My Uncle Jock (on the left) with my father, some time in the 1950s.

Harold's and my
wedding invitation.

Mrs. Ray Collier
requests the pleasure of your company
at the marriage of her daughter
June
to
Mr. Harold Kenton
at St. John's Wood Synagogue,
33 Abbey Road, N.W.8
on Sunday, 18th March, 1962
at 3 p.m.
and afterwards at
The Café Royal (Napoleon Suite)
Regent Street, W.1

R.S.V.P.
23 Middle Field,
St. John's Wood Park,   Reception 4.15 p.m.
        N.W.8   Dinner   5.30 p.m.

Harold and me setting
off to our wedding
reception, Sunday
18 March 1962.

My siblings before my arrival. L–R: Lewis, Helen and Gerald Collier, c. 1935. (Sunbeam Photo Ltd)

The earliest photo I have of myself, c. 1936 with my nanny of the time, Nanny Gray.

My first riding experience: Margate sea front, 1937. (Sunbeam Photo Ltd)

Playing in the garden in Newbury with my wonderful cousin Alan, c. 1942.

Me and my cousin Alan on our bikes in Newbury, c. 1942.

Setting off to Lillesden School
with my father in 1946.

Me on Gnome in 1950 at the
Benenden Riding Establishment.

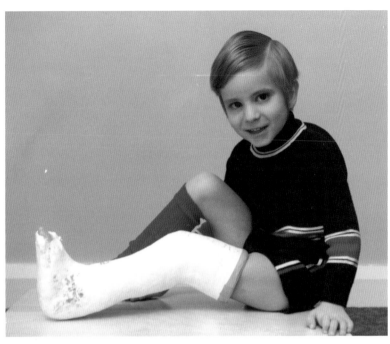

Our beautiful son, David, after his second operation on his foot when he was seven.

Our gorgeous little daughter, Jill, at around six months old.

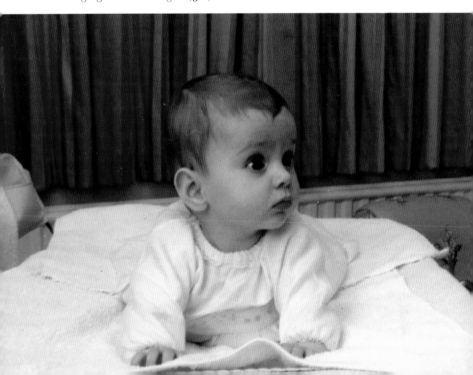

Cantsfield in Croydon: the Kenton family home for 35 years.

David and friends at his bar mitzvah party at Woburn Abbey, August 1978.

Our swimwear fashion parade on the streets of Knightsbridge, June 1978.

The cartoon from the *Evening Standard* that accompanied an article about Contour looking for a Middle Eastern Sales Rep. (© Ron McTrusty)

We copied the formula in Knightsbridge. We served drinks and canapés and we were all on hand to help. I will never forget one young man who made the most of the hospitality on offer and told me, in between hiccups, that he never knew buying knickers could be so much fun. And it was. We also sold naughty underwear at Christmas and, again, that proved to be successful.

Once there was a fault with a pair of crotchless knickers so Harold decided he would return them as he was going to the wholesaler later that day. Without thinking he put the knickers in his pocket, the better to remember them. On his way out he dropped into the shop to talk to me behind the counter. It was a busy day and there were quite a few customers milling around. Harold reached for his hankie and bought out the crotchless briefs from his pocket by mistake. It was hilarious and I couldn't work out who was more embarrassed, Harold, or Lady Whoever-She-Was who was standing by the till.

I do believe, though, that a lot of underwear is designed to be taken off. Often we would have a customer who would try on a bra that didn't fit very well but, in spite of the fact she was half falling out of it, she would love it. 'That's fine,' I would say. 'The perfect bedroom bra.'

One of my first solo press releases was on just this subject. We used to sell a lot of sexy underwear at Christmas, especially in Croydon, but more often than not it would be brought back before the New Year. 'I don't know why he bought this,' the woman would say. 'Not me at all.' She would then swap it for something practical. I thought it was sad because she hadn't got the message. He was saying: this is what I would like see you in rather than the boring 'büstenhalter' you wear every day. His purchase said, 'Let's have a bit of fun', but she exchanged it because it didn't fit or she thought it was too sexy.

We wanted our customers to be happy so, if the wife or girlfriend wanted something for everyday, we changed it. She went out with something she needed rather than what the man in her life wanted to see her wear. A pity, don't you think?

The issue made a good story and also generated lots of 'Letters to the Editor', which was perfect as far as we were concerned because everyone mentioned Contour and me. We got acres of press coverage, mostly along the lines of 'Croydon women aren't sexy'. And while I had exaggerated a little (of course I had) the point I was making was quite serious really.

We had decided by this stage that we needed to concentrate on Contour and thought it best to sell Manney's in Croydon and Manney's in Brixton. We made the sale harder for ourselves because we insisted that the two businesses needed to be sold as a package. We finally found a buyer and, while we did not make a great profit, we did celebrate because of what the market businesses had meant to us and, most of all, what they had taught us.

Then Harold had a brilliant idea – or at least we all thought it was. He decided that behind the fitting rooms in Knightsbridge we should set up a solarium and a travel agency. The thinking was that we could help our customers get a head start on their tans; and they could book their holiday flights at the same time. It took an enormous amount of effort to install the sun bed and the poor woman who ran Contour Travel had very little space, but for a while it was quite successful.

My next mission was another that was close to my heart. We frequently fitted young girls who, more often than not, came in with their mothers. I would strongly suggest that the mother stay outside the fitting room. 'Sit in the shop, have a cup of coffee, read a magazine and when we are ready, we'll call you.'

Some women did not get it.

If a mother is in the fitting room the teenager immediately gets stroppy and a fight breaks out. The young girl will challenge her mother over everything.

'I want a black bra,' is the usual starting point.

'No, darling. It's for school.' At this stage the mother is still quite patient.

'I can wear black bras to school.'

'No, you can't, darling.'

And so it goes on. If the mother makes the mistake of touching her daughter, all hell breaks loose. 'Don't interfere!' yells the child.

It really is so much easier for all concerned if the mother waits outside. We can say things to a girl that her mother cannot and, instead of a nightmare, the whole experience is enjoyable for everyone.

One day, I had been fitting a particularly stroppy young lady who was keen on sport. It made me think about all the young girls who might also be keen on sport but who did not get involved because their parents could not afford the right underwear. I was sure that there were a lot of girls who would not get undressed in a school changing room for fear of revealing their tatty bras.

You cannot do sport in the wrong bra because you bounce up and down which, apart from being embarrassing in front of the boys, can be painful. I was convinced that lots of youngsters would do more sport if only they had the right bra. I decided it would be fantastic if the daughters of people on income support could be given a bra voucher. I thought that would be state aid of a really useful kind.

Another press release came upon me. It was the time of Jim Callaghan's Labour government so I also shared my idea with Shirley Williams, who was Secretary of State for Education and Science at the time, as well as the Secretary of State for Social Services, David Ennals. It was David Ennals's office that arranged for me to receive a detailed reply from the Supplementary Benefits Commission.

The writer agreed that young girls did, indeed, need 'suitable brassieres' but explained that the subject could not be looked at in isolation as there were so many other groups of people who required special clothing.

> Whilst being sympathetic to the needs of all these persons, and fully appreciating their problems, I am afraid that with the limited resources available it is just not possible to extend the provisions of the National Health Service to them.
>
> However, young girls of poor families are not entirely without help in this matter. You may like to know that the basic supplementary benefit scale rates are intended to cover all normal requirements including the replacement of clothing of all kinds and footwear.

I was disappointed, but at least I had tried. Actually, I have tried several times since and I still think that a voucher specifically for bras for disadvantaged young girls would be an excellent thing, if any government were bold enough to introduce the idea.

My next promotion was less worthy but a lot more fun. Harold suggested that as we had such a large Arab clientele, we should think about sending a sales rep over to the Middle

East. 'That way,' he said, 'we could pick up the customers who don't come to London.' It was a joke, but a joke with potential. I ran off a press release saying we were looking for a rep 'with a certain amount of charm, charisma and social standing – a sort of Omar Sharif – to call on harems in the Middle East'.

Again we got acres of press coverage, but my favourite was an article that appeared in the People section of the *Evening Standard*:

Wanted: A Rep to sell 1001 Arabian Nighties
It's the sort of job you would think existed only in the fevered imaginations of hot-blooded males… selling underwear to the sultry occupants of Arabian harems. But not only is a London lingerie store advertising the post, it is offering a handsome salary of £5,000 plus commission. Would-be applicants are faced with one major drawback, however. Oversexed monolinguists will not be considered.

'We are looking for someone who is Arabic speaking; not necessarily an Arab, but a person who knows their ways,' said Mr Harold Kenton, Managing Director of Contour of Knightsbridge. 'Also he must be able to behave himself; we don't want a eunuch on our hands.'

Mr Kenton conceived the idea of an Arabian nightie salesman after his shop did brisk business with Eastern ladies visiting London. 'We learned from our customers that the harem is still very common out there, and we thought if we were going to do any multiple business it was worth having a man on the spot covering the Gulf States,' he said.

The successful applicant will be expected to mix in the wealthier circles – a large harem is a symbol of riches – introduce himself to husbands, and then win the confidence of the head wife, traditionally the female ruler of the harem.

A strong constitution will be needed to handle the drinking that goes with the job. 'And there are other lavish entertainments,' said Mr Kenton darkly. Arabs have marked tastes in underwear, he says. 'They definitely don't go for stockings and suspenders and see-through nylon stuff. They really only go for the world's best. Handmade silk nightdresses, sexy satins and beautiful lace.'

That doesn't come cheap. Pure silk negligees in Mr Kenton's store sell for £250.

The copy was accompanied by a wonderful drawing by the cartoonist Ron McTrusty. I loved it so much that I bought the original and had it framed along with a clipping of the article: it hung in our office for years. It was an excellent reminder of what you can achieve with a bit of imagination, a typewriter and a first-class stamp.

CHAPTER FIVE

Not long after we moved to Croydon I joined the newly formed local branch of WIZO, the Women's International Zionist Organisation. It is a little like the Women's Institute, but without the jam, and with a very different take on Jerusalem. WIZO is a voluntary organisation dedicated to social welfare and we do all sorts of things to raise money for Israel and have a social life at the same time.

Croydon was not north London and I wanted to be part of a network of Jewish mums. We all had young children and it was great to leave our husbands at home to babysit while we got together once a month to organise fund-raising events.

At one of our meetings there was to be a speaker called Doreen Gainsford, one of the founding members of the Women's Campaign for Soviet Jewry. Little did I know when I set off to hear Doreen speak that, by the end of the evening, I would be a different woman. I could never have imagined that I would spend much of the next twenty years on the streets.

Doreen spoke passionately and vividly about how tough life was in Russia if you were Jewish. She told us that the 1967 Arab-Israeli Six Day War had sparked a rush of applications from Soviet Jews who wanted to go to Israel. Some were allowed to leave, but the thousands who were not became known as 'refuseniks'. Doreen spoke about the work being done in the USSR and abroad to help the refuseniks, who faced considerable hardship, but explained that more needed to be done. Then she told us about a woman called Sylva Zalmanson.

Sylva was Latvian and her husband, Eduard Kuznetzov, was Russian. Both were Jewish, both were activists (Eduard had already served seven years in prison for his political views) and both wanted to emigrate to Israel. They applied for an exit visa knowing that the consequences were potentially disastrous. They knew that many of the Jews who had applied were treated as 'traitors to Mother Russia' and had lost their jobs and their incomes. If the refuseniks were lucky, they could find menial work and scratch out a living; if not, they risked being accused of being 'parasites', as at that time it was illegal to be without employment in the USSR. What was equally frightening was that the simple act of applying to emigrate generated the KGB's interest. That, in turn, could lead to harassment and even imprisonment.

When Eduard and Sylva's application to emigrate to Israel was denied they came up with a bold, and ultimately, foolhardy plan to bring the refuseniks' plight to the attention of the world. In conjunction with a qualified pilot (frustrated at not being able to find a job that matched his experience) and nine others (including two of Sylva's brothers), they plotted to hijack a plane at Leningrad airport and fly to Sweden. So they booked seats on the small plane, supposedly because they were going to a wedding, and everything was carefully planned. But the group was betrayed and, before they could even board the aircraft, they were arrested. That was Wednesday 3 June, 1970.

In the closed trial that followed, Eduard Kuznetzov and the pilot, Mark Dymshitz, were sentenced to death and the others to varying terms of imprisonment. Sylva, the only woman to be tried and only twenty-six years old at the time, was sentenced to ten years' hard labour – to include six months of solitary confinement.

The troubles the Soviet Jews faced were already known about internationally, but the fate of those involved in 'Operation Wedding' sparked almost instant worldwide protest. In London, Amelie Jakobovits, the wife of the Chief Rabbi, led a march of the Association of Women's Jewish Organisations to the Soviet Embassy, and similar marches were held around the world. The Kremlin obviously took notice: the death sentences were commuted to life imprisonment (later reduced again to fifteen years) and the zeal of campaigners was ignited afresh.

Doreen also told us about a consul at the Israeli Embassy in charge of Soviet Jewish Affairs. Ijo Rager, inspired by the 'Operation Wedding' protest march, decided that Jewish women were an untapped source. He has since been reported as saying, 'I felt it was the women in the community who had the time to devote to the cause. The students, who up to then were the only active force for Soviet Jewry, were busy with their studies. The men had little free time and the Jewish Establishment was very cool about the movement. I saw that women activists could be a good gimmick.'

Ijo Rager was right, but he knew that nice girls did not take to the streets – especially not nice Jewish girls. When he heard about the troubles of a young Odessa librarian, Raiza Palatnik, who had been imprisoned for 'slandering the Soviet Union', when all she had done was apply to leave Russia, he picked up the phone. Ijo invited three women to meet him – Barbara Oberman, Doreen Gainsford and Joan Dale.

At that stage, Raiza Palatnik was on a hunger strike in protest against the appalling conditions in which she was being held. Raiza was thirty-five years old. The London women, who were of a similar age, decided that thirty-five of them would stage their own hunger strike outside the Russian Embassy in Bayswater and would deliver a letter to the wife of the Russian ambassador asking her to help Raiza. Joan Dale suggested they should wear black and it was agreed a silent protest would be the most powerful.

The protest went ahead as planned and from a nearby phone box Doreen, a professional publicist, set to work. She rang every newspaper, television and radio station she could think of to tell them that, 'we are a group of thirty-five girls, demonstrating outside the Soviet Embassy for the release of a Jewish woman imprisoned because she wants to go to Israel. She is thirty-five years of age and we are here for thirty-five hours in a sympathy hunger strike.'

Doreen said that it was during one of her phone calls that she heard someone on the *Daily Telegraph* news desk say, 'It's those thirty-fives again'. The name stuck.

In a fascinating book, *Those Wonderful Women in Black*, by Daphne Gerlis, Barbara Oberman also relates her memories of that day. 'We were all so naïve; during our hunger strike the father of one of the group drove up in his Rolls-Royce with food for "the starving girls". We had to ask him to disappear – fast…'

Barbara goes on to recall that in the afternoon they received a message from Ijo at the Israeli Embassy saying that, 'Raiza has already been moved from a KGB dungeon to an ordinary prison in Odessa.' How powerful is that?

Doreen, and what she had to say, changed my life. It was as if someone had lit a bulb inside me. What she expressed is what I felt. Like many people of my generation, I felt guilty that my parents had not done anything to help their fellow Jews during the Second World War. The more I learned about the horrors of the Holocaust, the more I felt they should have done something – anything. I don't know if they knew about the unspeakable horrors the Nazis had inflicted on Jewish people, but if not, why not? When Doreen explained about what was happening to the Jews in the Soviet Union, I thought, 'I really have to do what I can'. I knew I could not face the idea that David and Jill might ask, 'Why didn't you do something?'

So, I did do something. I became a '35er'.

My first demonstration was during a Georgian State Dance Company show at the Fairfield Halls in Croydon. I organised a group of us, including some of my non-Jewish friends, to protest outside the halls and hand out leaflets explaining what was happening to the Jews in the Soviet Union. It was very successful and we got a fair amount of publicity. I knew I had found my true vocation.

My next call was to get a group of twelve together to go to Selhurst Park Stadium, the home ground of Crystal Palace Football Club, where Leningrad was due to play. We were to dress as footballers, each of us wearing the name of a refusenik. We got our outfits sorted and put black coats over the top so we would not be rumbled. We bought our tickets for the match and waited. (If we were going into a venue we always did it legally, and we would stage our protest at the beginning or end of an event so as not to upset the spectators.) When the Leningrad team came out onto the pitch, the twelve of us dropped our coats and climbed over the fence. The funniest thing was that, in the beginning, the Russians were excited because they thought we were a fan club! We handed the Leningrad captain a letter about what was going on in his homeland just before security pounced and escorted us out via the tunnel.

Harold was on the other side of the fence to collect our coats and meet us once we had been kicked out of the ground.

We had men who supported the 35s but Harold was the only husband who was a constant support. Wherever we were we could always count on Harold.

I was thrown out of many places during my campaigning career but Selhurst Park was the first. David was so jealous. He could not care less that his mother had been thrown out, but he was green with envy that she had been down the tunnel at Crystal Palace!

Life fell into a bizarre routine. Whenever there was a Russian presence in London, the 35s would be there. I became the south London organiser and when I heard that the Russian tennis star, Olga Morozova, was going to defend her title at the Beckenham Green Shield tennis tournament, I decided to be there with another one of our members. As Olga finished her match I stepped out onto the court. I presented her with a bunch of flowers with a note pleading for help for the imprisoned Sylva Zalmanson. The very next day there was a lovely photo of Olga smiling as she received the flowers from me on the front page of the *Daily Express*. I suspect her minders would not have been smiling when they read the accompanying article, because it told the story of why we had pulled the stunt.

We made the front page of the *Daily Express* again a couple of months later when we raced onto the ice to present Sylva Zalmanson medals to the Russian skaters who were taking part in the International Ice Dancing Championships in Streatham. It was great publicity even if the photo the paper used was a little unbecoming. As I raced out onto the ice I slipped and fell flat on my back – and that is what made the front page. Mind you, the story explained that the note accompanying the medals read, 'Please wear these medallions to help obtain the release of a prisoner of conscience.' I was sore for weeks but knowing we had made the front page, yet again, helped me feel better.

While we were busy in south London they were also hard at it in north London and barely a month would go by without some inventive protest or other. (Soon there were 35s groups all over the country.) We were effective but it was not easy, especially because the Jewish establishment did not approve of what we were doing. In fact, they were dead against us. It was considered irresponsible for law-abiding, respectable, middle-class women to be involved in such indignities. We were also told, quite firmly, that if we made too much noise about what was happening in Russia we would stir up anti-Semitism in Britain. What rubbish!

The Russians did not like adverse publicity and we made sure they got a lot. We also ran a very important scheme of ringing the refuseniks on a regular basis. It was well known that if a refusenik had connections in the West, he or she would be unlikely to just 'disappear'. Along with a friend, Ruth Urban, I took on the job of making regular phone calls to the Smeliansky family in Moscow. Emanuel Smeliansky was a metallurgical engineer and the minute he applied to leave he lost his job and had to take work as a night watchman. Life was very hard for him, his wife Alla and their young son, Mischa. Emanuel could not speak English but Alla could, and Ruth and I took it in turns to ring once a month. We rang Alla Smeliansky for seventeen years!

Looking back now, I wonder how we managed to do everything we did, alongside looking after our families and, in my case, helping to run the business; but we were all driven.

David and Jill were often involved and that was good because they learned that life is not just about living in a beautiful house and came to understand that everything in the world isn't hunky dory. I was very proud when David decided he wanted to share his bar mitzvah, by proxy, with a young Russian boy, Edward Besprozvany, who lived in what was then Leningrad, now (once again) St Petersburg. We sent Edward a present and David wrote to him to tell him all about the service. It was lovely.

Both our children were so good, and Jill was terrific when we were out and about. If we were handing out leaflets and someone threw one away, she would pick it up and run after them, 'You dropped this,' she would say sweetly and hand it back to them. It worked every time.

I also had tremendous support from our local members of parliament. John Moore was MP for Croydon Central and Bernard Wetherill was the MP for Croydon North East. Neither was Jewish but both became good friends and did everything they could to support the 35s. Before entering politics Bernard had worked in the family tailoring business and, although he had long since moved on, he still carried his tailoring thimble in his pocket. He said it was a reminder of his origins and the need for humility, no matter how high one rises. He was a lovely man. John too was lovely and was also very good looking. Everyone used to go on about his film-star looks!

John and Bernard joined us in September 1974 at my house when Sylva Zalmanson was released. We had heard that, entirely without warning, she had been let out of prison and told to leave Russia. The 35s saw it as an unprecedented victory over the Soviet system. It was the first time, to our knowledge, that anyone had been released from a prison camp before serving their full term. It was fantastic.

We took heart, but we did not celebrate – there was still too much to do. Sylva went straight to Israel, but the following year she came to London to personally thank the 35s for all we had done on her behalf and to encourage us to fight on for her husband and brothers. Our work was far from over.

We enlisted help from the local churches and the Bishop of Croydon, the Right Reverend John Hughes, was terrific. The Bishop understood injustice. On one occasion I got him up to the LBC studios in London to do a broadcast about Soviet Jewry. When we got there he said, 'I don't think I can do this.'

'You can,' I said, 'and you will.'

He argued that I should do it, but we both knew that if he did the interview it would be more powerful. He did do it, and it was.

We also had wonderful support and understanding from Lady Carrington, whose husband was Foreign Secretary between 1979 and 1982. She was a customer of mine at Contour and was a hugely sympathetic woman. When I knew her husband was due to go to Moscow, she told me to write to her about the Smeliansky family and she would see what she could do. I did, and received the most wonderful reply from the Foreign Office. They explained that Lord Carrington knew about the Smelianskys and their difficulties and their case had already been taken up with the appropriate authorities. As regards his latest trip to Moscow, which was very short, they said:

> We gave a good deal of thought to whether Lord Carrington should raise individual examples of abuse of human rights such as that of your family. But we decided that it would have been invidious to choose from the very many deserving cases which have come to our attention. Lord Carrington therefore decided to raise the issue in general terms. He reminded

Mr Gromyko [Soviet Minister of Foreign Affairs] of the importance which the Government attaches to human rights and of the strong feeling in the United Kingdom on this subject, including the question of Soviet Jews.

We shall of course keep up the pressure on behalf of all those in the Soviet Union who suffer repression because of their wish to enjoy fundamental human rights and freedom, including the Smeliansky family. We can only hope that there will be better news of them soon.

Not a bad letter, I thought, for a bra-fitter from Croydon to receive!

We had so much support from all sections of society that when I came across resistance to what we were fighting for I was amazed. There is one particular incident that sticks in my mind – and in my throat. Harold and I had been invited to dinner with friends and there was a gentleman there whom we had not met before. He was very boring and went on and on about his flying exploits. I only sat up and took notice when he mentioned that he and several other guests had been at the Royal Opera House in Covent Garden that day. I knew that the 35s had been there too, handing out leaflets to the people in the queue, because it was where the Bolshoi Ballet was due to perform.

I thought my fellow dinner guest was about to say how wonderful it was that the Women's Campaign for Soviet Jewry was so conscientious. Far from it. 'There we were trying to buy tickets and here were these women protesting about what was happening to Jews in Russia. It was ridiculous. I've never been so embarrassed.'

Harold was sitting opposite me and I could feel him praying that I wouldn't say anything. I did. 'You,' I said, looking directly at the man, 'are the most disgusting person I've ever met.'

My outburst did rather disturb the dinner party and it took a while for my friend, whose house we were in, to forgive me. But I was so angry, especially because the man who had dismissed our efforts was Jewish.

What made his comment even more sickening was that we knew we were making a difference. We wrote thousands upon thousands of cards and letters to politicians, church leaders, diplomats – anyone we thought could further the cause. We also sent countless cards, letters and parcels to the USSR. Most were never received but as Daphne Gerlis points out in *Those Wonderful Women in Black*, '…they were seen by the KGB and other officials, serving to remind them of the West's unflagging support of the refuseniks'.

Our small Croydon group was particularly creative; we came up with all sorts of stunts. We converted an empty shop in Croydon into a prison and served cabbage soup to passers-by; we had Lady Godiva on a horse riding around London (in a modest body stocking I must add); we sent parcels of 'matzoh' to little Mischa Smeliansky at Passover; and on one occasion we invaded the Lada stand at Earls Court during the motor show. We had been told that a refusenik had been deliberately run over by the KGB, so one of us lay down in front of the display car while the rest of us locked ourselves inside. We were there for about an hour and stirred up a lot of interest. When we finally let ourselves out we were approached by the KGB guys on the stand (whenever there was a Russian anything in the UK there were always KGB men around). We expected them to escort us out of the show with a flea in our ears and couldn't believe it when they asked if we could come back the following day. It turned out they had never had so many people on the Lada stand before!

One of my favourite stunts was when a friend of mine, Barbara Benjamin, and I went to Wimbledon because the Russian tennis star Teimuraz Kakulia was playing. Barbara and I were dressed normally but had Wombles costumes in our bag. As the match was going on we slipped behind a shed and changed. Kakulia won his match and as he did so we slipped through the security cordon (you couldn't do that these days), unfurled our banner and presented Kakulia with a token rubbish bag. Inside the bag was an important message: 'The Wombles of Wimbledon clean up litter from the streets of Great Britain. The KGB of the USSR remove Jews from the streets.' At first Kakulia was thrilled because he thought we were there to congratulate him, but his minders knew differently and quickly spirited him away. Once again, we were thrown out, but we made several front pages in the press the following day so all was good.

What was also good was the courtesy we received from the police. They were phenomenal. Once twenty-two of us, each wearing the name of a different refusenik, chained ourselves to the railings outside the Foreign Office and tucked the padlock keys inside our bras. The police had to cut the chains before they could arrest us and the senior policeman said that every 'prisoner' had to have her own constable (mine was a very pleasant man called George). George invited me into the police van or Black Mariah and escorted me to the station. I was getting a little worried because I had to collect Jill from school and George explained this to the sergeant. 'Right,' said the boss, 'we'll deal first with those of you who have to pick up kids from school.' And that is what they did.

The next morning we appeared at the Bow Street Magistrates Court and I had to suppress my giggles when the magistrate asked to see the evidence. All you could hear was the clank of chains! We were all bound over to keep the peace for a year, which the magistrate thought (incorrectly) would curb our activities, but I was the only one not worried about what my husband would say. Harold was the only husband who came to court that day and he was not remotely cross because he believed totally in what I was doing.

There was also one very memorable occasion when Harold played an active part. By this time Doreen Gainsford had, herself, emigrated to Israel and another wonderful, dynamic woman had taken charge of the campaign. Rita Eker was as tireless as her predecessor and is still an inspiration. Rita came up with a plan for the opening night of the Russian State Dancers' performance at the Coliseum in London. We pre-booked all the boxes and the entire front row and painted up scores of umbrellas with the names of different refuseniks.

The plan was that we would take our seats and at an agreed signal, the blast of a hunting horn, we would all stand and open our umbrellas. We got to a nearby hotel early to run through the plan and that is when Rita discovered that the musician she had booked to sound the hunting horn had cold feet: he was concerned his union would not approve of him taking part. Rita turned to Harold. 'Can you play a horn?' she asked him.

'Rita, I'm in the knicker business,' he said. 'What would I know of hunting horns?'

'Don't worry, you soon will. It can't be that difficult.' Rita asked the reluctant horn player to show Harold what to do. The two men disappeared downstairs to the Gents, where they could use a toilet bowl as a muffle, and Harold reappeared just before it was time to go on to the theatre and take our places.

It amused me when a little waitress came to our box to ask if we would like to order drinks for the interval. 'No thank you. I don't think so,' I said trying hard not to smile – I knew we would be getting thrown out long before we could enjoy any refreshments. Seconds before the show was about to start, Harold stood up and gave a mighty blast on the horn. As one, the rest of us stood up, pulled our brollies out from under our coats and unfurled them. It was wonderful. We made all the papers and *The Times* not only reported on our protest, mentioning Harold's blast of the hunting horn in particular, but it was also the basis of their next day's cartoon.

Over the years, prisoners such as the jailed dissident Anatoly Shcharansky became a 'cause célèbre', but we also campaigned for hundreds and hundreds of lesser-known refuseniks and prisoners. Anatoly (who on release adopted the Hebrew name Natan, and simplified the spelling of his surname to Sharansky) went on to become an Israeli politician and activist. His moving book of his experiences, *Fear No Evil*, served to strengthen our resolve.

The 35s fought on.

We became very worried about Emanuel Smeliansky as his wife, Alla, said he was very depressed and had threatened to commit suicide in Red Square. We and our friends Ruth and Richard Urban, who were part of the telephone chain, decided we needed to go to Moscow. Various 35ers had made the trip previously and we were well advised what to do.

We booked a trip with Thomson's Holidays , applied for our visas and started collecting what we were told would be appreciated – jeans, nail varnish, biros, chewing gum, 'siddurs' and various medications. Harold, who had never been to a doctor in his life, knew that if he was asked he had to pretend the pills were his. He was especially nervous because he struggled to remember what was meant to be the matter with him and what the pills were for!

We were prepared to have our luggage checked when we got to Moscow but, luckily, because the weather was so awful, there was a delay and several flights arrived at once. Only one of our cases, the one that contained the prayer books, was opened, but when we said they were Chinese texts, and not at all important, we were waved through.

We joined a tour with the Thomson's group around the Kremlin but otherwise we did our own thing as much as we could get away with. It was absolutely wonderful to meet Alla and Emanuel face-to-face and we also met up with several other refuseniks and Soviet Jewish activists. We had strict instructions not to talk in our hotel bedroom (Harold loved that order as it meant I couldn't talk to him) and we were absolutely forbidden from writing down anything – anything at all. If we wanted to talk we had to go into the bathroom and flush the toilet or run the taps. It was madness. There was a woman on each floor who monitored everyone's comings and goings. I don't know if it was because we gave our woman chewing gum, but we had no trouble at all.

Our contacts came to collect us from the hotel, supposedly to show us around the city, and we gave them things from our luggage. We handed over the drugs which were needed in Siberia and took verbal requests for new necessities. It was on an underground train (suitably noisy) that one of our contacts gave Harold a verbal prescription for spectacles which he had to remember. (When we got home the glasses were duly made according to the prescription he had memorised and were conveyed back to Moscow with the next group of 35 travellers.) We were only in Moscow for a few days but when we left we had only the clothes we were wearing: our cases were completely empty. It was the most amazing time, really amazing. We all felt we had done something of true worth.

A short while later, the Smeliansky family was finally granted permission to leave Russia. They were over the moon but, if I am honest, I felt betrayed. I was thrilled they could leave, of course I was, but they chose not to go to Israel. Their son Mischa wanted to train as a doctor and Alla and Emanuel thought his chances in Canada would be better. I thought that, considering all we had done for them, they owed Israel a couple of years at the very least.

Then suddenly (or so it seemed to me) the world changed. On Thursday 9 November 1989 the Berlin Wall was pulled down and we prayed that the fall of the Soviet Union would not be far behind. It was not. A mere thirteen months later Mikhail Gorbachev resigned as president and the hammer and sickle flag was lowered for the last time. The USSR was dead.

Only then did we allow ourselves to celebrate.

Daphne Gerlis, in *Those Wonderful Women in Black*, records various testimonials to the work of the 35s, but the one that affects me most is that of John Simpson, then Foreign Affairs Editor of the BBC (now World Affairs Editor of the BBC).

> I think the 35s played a distinguished part during the late 1970s and 1980s in the process which led to the collapse of communism. For one thing, they supported and drew attention to the one process, which, more than all others, brought about change in the old Soviet Union: the discontent which most educated people there, a great many of them Jewish, felt towards the State itself. This made it inevitable that the State would have to change. By encouraging Soviet

Jews to think about emigration, supporting their claims, I believe the Women's Campaign added significantly to this process.

Secondly, the 35s kept up an important and noticeable campaign in Britain after Gorbachev had come to power, prodding the consciences of politicians and journalists so that they would not forget what was still going on in the Soviet Union. Once Gorbachev had made his mark, it was very easy to think that everything was now all right with the Soviet Union, when it clearly wasn't. What the 35s did wasn't always popular at the time because people liked Gorbachev and wanted to believe that Moscow had changed. I think that by reminding us that it hadn't changed nearly enough, they did a great deal of good. And in the end the people of Russia themselves showed that they didn't feel things had changed enough either.

The 35s have a great deal to be proud of in their campaign. Their approach to the media was always intelligent and they used us in exactly the right way. As for me, I am very glad to have been in contact with the 35s over the years. Of all the pressure groups I've dealt with I think they were the best and most effective.

What more can I say?

CHAPTER SIX

Contour continued to do well – very well. We had built up a loyal customer base, in both Croydon and Knightsbridge, and we never missed an opportunity to attract new business.

We came up with promotions on a regular basis and when, on 24 February 1981, the engagement of Prince Charles to Lady Diana Spencer was officially announced, we sprang into action. We quickly found the nightdress and negligee set that we had put away three years earlier and, as per Ivor's instructions, legged it over to Buckingham Palace to deliver a beautifully wrapped box for Lady Diana.

I sent out the press release and photo, confident that it would result in a fair few column inches. On the back of the photo was a label which said that the nightwear set had been 'specially designed for Contour of Knightsbridge'. The phrase was repeated in most of the press articles.

We got a very gracious letter from the Palace thanking us for the lovely gift, but the very same day we received another letter that was not so heart-warming. It was from the solicitors of the company who had supplied the nightwear set we had sent to the palace.

Whoops!

They were upset that we had said it was 'specially designed for Contour' because it was not. We had bought it from them, that was not in question, but it was not an exclusive set. The company threatened to sue.

I would be lying if I said we weren't worried. We were very worried, but Harold's cousin, Bernard Pentel, who was a solicitor, came to our rescue. I cannot remember what he did, but Bernard sorted it out. He saved us a lot of money and a lot of embarrassment.

I was more cautious with the next story I relayed to the papers.

Harrods in those days was owned by the House of Fraser Group and in 1981 the company undertook to install more escalators to supplement the only one that was in the shop. Luckily for us, the first new escalator led up to the store from Harrods' Door Ten, which is immediately opposite what was then Contour's front door. We thought it very generous that House of Fraser's modernisation programme boosted our passing trade and, of course, put out a press release saying exactly that.

We were very busy and for Harold that meant a lot of toing and froing between home, the Whitgift Centre and Knightsbridge. If at all possible Harold would use the trains rather than drive but there was one particular occasion when I think he regretted his choice of transport. He had had a particularly hectic day and, as per normal, climbed on the train to come home in the evening carrying a briefcase full of the day's takings. Harold arrived at Croydon and got off the train but, unfortunately, the briefcase did not. The case continued on to Eastbourne. I confess I was not overly sympathetic when my sometimes absent-minded husband rang to tell me what had happened, but it was amazing how it all worked out. The Station Master at Croydon rang the Station Master at Eastbourne who not only retrieved the case, but personally delivered it back to Harold, who had waited at Croydon station. We were so relieved and the minute Harold got home we did a count. (In those days we counted the takings every night to make sure they tallied with the till receipts.) Usually the tally was spot on, or sometimes a few pence under, but this time we had more money in hand than the till receipts said we should have had! Harold's forgetfulness may have caused a few hours of anxiety but it did not cost us a single penny and seemed to have earned us a bob or two. It was fantastic.

We were also lucky a short while later when Harold had another little bout of absent-mindedness. We were woken at midnight one night by the police ringing to ask where we were. 'Fast asleep in bed,' said Harold.

'That's interesting, Sir,' said the policeman, 'because I'm ringing you from your shop in Knightsbridge. All the lights are on, the door is open and I'm standing by the counter. You may wish, Sir, to come back down and lock up.'

I have never seen Harold move so quickly. He threw on some clothes, leapt down the stairs and was in the car and off before I had a chance to even compute what had happened. Yet once again, we were so lucky. Nothing at all had been taken. It seems that the only person who decided to come into the shop that night was the friendly policeman who gave us a call.

Harold was more attentive after that for a while but, in truth, he had so much to think about and worked so hard that he sometimes forgot the practicalities of life – Harold and keys, for instance, were never destined to have a long-term relationship.

While we were busy with the shops, David and Jill had been busy at school. David started at Dulwich Preparatory and then went on to a wonderful school called Cumner House, because we were worried that he would not pass his Eleven

Plus. Cumner had really excellent teachers, and not only did David pass his exams, but he was offered a place at Dulwich College, another at Whitgift School and won a scholarship to Carmel College, a Jewish secondary school in Wallingford.

I had loved boarding school (it really was the making of me) and I wanted the children to have the same opportunity. We chose Carmel for two reasons. Firstly, my Uncle Jock had been good friends with the founder, Rabbi Kopul Rosen, and had paid for the school synagogue to be built, so there was a family connection. Secondly, we wanted the children to be educated in a Jewish environment because in Croydon we were not in the wider Jewish community. We were miles from a synagogue and if we wanted kosher meat or challah we had to go to north London. The trip always involved a bulk-buy and I would freeze what we did not need there and then for future weeks.

When I went to board at Lillesden as a young girl, it was my first experience of non-Jewish life. For David and Jill, Carmel College offered the complete opposite. Unfortunately, the school closed in 1997, but during the 1980s it provided our children with an excellent education in academic subjects as well as Jewish lore and tradition.

I always hoped that David would go to university but he was not remotely interested. All he wanted to do was work with cars. David has been car mad since he was a little boy – he never went anywhere without a car in hand and could not wait to learn to drive. Many years later, when he was in thirties, he and his father built a Caterham car (a lightweight sports car) together in David's garage at Stanmore. Harold used to insist that he was very useful indeed, but our son has yet to forget that his father managed to drop the engine on his foot – David's foot, that is, not his own. (Thank God for steel toe-cap boots!) David still has his Caterham and still drives it when he fancies a trip down memory lane.

It just so happened that when David was ready to finish school, we had a customer whose husband was in the motor industry. What's more, he had known my parents so, after a word here and a word there, David went to work with Lex Garages.

At around the same time that David started work we celebrated Jill's 'bat mitzvah'. It is a relatively new celebration (it began in the 1920s in America) but has become popular everywhere. It is, if nothing else, a great excuse for a party, and we *love* parties.

The rules of the synagogue are strict: girls do not play a part in the service. What normally happens for a bat mitzvah ceremony is that at the end of the Sabbath service on Saturday morning, the girl in question goes up onto the steps, gives a 'Dvar Torah', and later is presented with a cookbook.

Jill's bat mitzvah, we thought, should be something more.

If she had needed an Evelyn Rose cookbook – because it usually was Evelyn Rose's *Complete Jewish Cookery* that was given to girls in those days – we would have bought her one. How much better to have something more important, like a siddur that you could use every Sabbath. And I wanted Jill to take part in the service and to sing. (Jill has the loveliest voice.) I am not sure that the Rabbi was particularly impressed, but we arranged a special service to be held on Jill's actual twelfth birthday, Sunday 14 February 1982. And it was special.

It was even more special for me because Rosalind Runcie, the wife of the Archbishop of Canterbury at the time, came to the ceremony. Rosalind and I had become friends during the Royal Marsden campaign (I'll tell you about that later) and I was thrilled that she accepted the invitation to come to Jill's bat mitzvah.

After the service at Catford Synagogue, the synagogue we belonged to at the time, we all went to the most fabulous hotel in Surrey. Selsdon Park is a beautiful seventeenth-century manor house and they served us the most fantastic tea. As if that was not enough, the following week we invited all the same friends and family, plus a few, for a dinner cruise up the Thames, complete with a jazz band. Even Jill, who has a passion for parties, agrees that she came of age in style.

A few months later, out of the blue, we received a phone call from a woman called Tessa Seidon who owned a bespoke corsetry company called Rigby & Peller. She wanted to sell it. Mrs Seidon was not well and the business was struggling; there were loads of gaps in the order book. Mrs Seidon knew about Contour and asked if we would be interested in buying her out. Harold thought not, I was not sure.

We agreed to go to Mayfair to have a look.

Rigby & Peller straddled three past-their-glory floors in South Moulton Street, off Oxford Street. (There was a tiny salon on the first floor and workrooms above.) There was no street frontage to speak of and little to indicate what the company did. The biggest selling point, in fact the only selling point, was that Rigby & Peller had a Royal Warrant: the company had provided bespoke corsetry to the Queen for twenty-two years.

Many years earlier, in 1939, a Hungarian refugee, Gita Peller, had arrived in London and found lodgings with a woman called Bertha Rigby. Gita was one of about 50,000 Jewish refugees who escaped the rising flood of fascism in Europe during the 1930s and sought refuge in the United Kingdom. She was an accomplished corsetiere and, by coincidence, so was the equally nimble-fingered Mrs Rigby. The two women decided to go into business together and took on the premises in South Moulton Street.

The commercial production of ready-to-wear bras had taken off in the 1930s but, for the women who could afford it, made-to-measure underwear remained the preferred option. My mother, for example, always had her bras and corsets made for her by a wonderful woman called Madame Illa Knina.

As an aside, Illa was also half Hungarian (her mother was Czech) and was an excellent businesswoman as well as a superb seamstress. Her passion, outside of work, was art. She had a fantastic eye and collected pieces from the up-and-coming artists of the day. One of Illa's heroes was the entertainer Frankie Vaughan. When she was well into her eighties, Illa invited him to come to meet her because she admired not only his voice, but all he did for the National Association of Boys' Clubs. (As a little boy Frankie Abelson, as he was then, had been a member of the Lancaster Lads' Club.) Mummy told me that when Illa Knina died she left the Association £4 million – the proceeds of her art collection – inspired as she was by Mr Vaughan's example.

I do not know if Illa Knina ever met her rivals Gita Peller and Bertha Rigby, but it is not unlikely considering the small world in which they worked and the fact that Illa's salon was in Bruton Street – a mere few hundred yards away from Rigby & Peller's salon.

In 1956 Tessa Seidon, Gita Peller's niece, took on the business. Four years later Mrs Seidon became the Grantee of the Royal Warrant and Rigby & Peller officially became corsetieres to Queen Elizabeth II. (Someone from the company would have been going to the palace before that, mind you, because you cannot apply for a Royal Warrant until you have served for a minimum of five years and can provide receipts to prove the point.)

Mrs Seidon was a not a natural businesswoman and I suspect she would never have taken on Rigby & Peller had she not inherited it. After twenty-six years she had had more than enough and wanted to be rid of it.

Harold decided he was not interested. I decided the exact opposite. 'How, Harold,' I said, 'can you turn down the Royal Warrant?'

'Easily,' said my never-ever-argumentative husband. 'Very easily. We don't need Rigby & Peller. I don't want Rigby & Peller. We can't afford Rigby & Peller.'

We bought Rigby & Peller.

Once we knew I could succeed Mrs Seidon as the Queen's corsetiere, we handed over £20,000 and took on the last made-to-measure corsetry business in the UK. We inherited years of shabbiness and chipped paintwork as well as drawer upon drawer of beautiful lace and beribboned gorgeousness, much of which was long out of date. (Several items went to the Victoria & Albert Museum and the rest I stored in silk-lined suitcases for the rainy day that I knew would come.)

We also inherited four seamstresses and the one and only Gerda Oblath. Gerda had been Mrs Seidon's assistant and was an amazing woman: a very capable German perfectionist. Gerda did everything, and anything, well and eventually became our secretary.

Initially, other than a little much-needed tidying and titivating, we left Rigby & Peller to continue with made-to-measure. We did introduce some ready-to-wear but we needed to get more bespoke customers to keep the workroom busy.

Generously endowed genteel country ladies, many real Ladies (with a proper capital L), were the backbone of the business, alongside the crème de la crème of London's aristocracy. One of the firm's most loyal customers was Princess Margaret, who never put anything on in terms of underwear or swimwear that wasn't Rigby & Peller. The Princess needed a lot of swimwear because she was often in Mustique and Mrs Seidon told me that she was particularly fond of the 'Lollobrigida look' (boned and waspish), but I thought something a little more modern might be suitable. After several visits to Kensington Palace, I plucked up the courage to take some samples of what I had in mind. I laid out on the bed several lovely lycra-rich swimsuits and cover-ups. The Princess was not impressed. 'I could not wear those,' she sneered, 'they're synthetic.'

She insisted that she only wanted, and would only wear, swimsuits that we made especially for her to her preferred style and in her preferred fabric. I decided it best not to mention that everything we made for her contained nylon!

The Princess did not suffer fools gladly – or otherwise – and was very aware of her status. I warmed to her more years later, when I learned that she was very supportive of Princess Diana.

Irrespective of what I thought of Princess Margaret, it was clear we needed more customers like her. The solution was more press releases. More press releases; more column inches; more trade. Everyone knows that people want good service and that is what we built our reputation on. Good service is the most important thing in business. You will go back to someone who serves you well and is helpful.

We made sure we were particularly helpful, and I have the most wonderful collection of letters to support the claim. No request was too small. The novelist Barbara Cartland, or Dame Barbara Cartland as she became, was a case in point.

She never came in to Rigby & Peller but she would ring up, or her dresser would ring up, and ask for such things as twelve corset buttons or half a dozen hooks and eyes. She treated us like a corsetry haberdashers and I never remember her being fitted for a bra or a girdle or anything of substance.

I do remember, though, that every now and again she would send photographs of herself swathed in pink and signed, 'With love from Barbara'.

She was an extraordinary woman. I can't say I have ever read one of her books, but as she wrote more than seven hundred, which sold in the hundreds of millions, I must be an exception. (I believe she was in the *Guinness Book of Records*, and maybe still is, for having written twenty-six in a single year!)

One Rigby & Peller customer whom I loved immediately was Dawn French. She is every bit as much fun as you think she will be. She is just gorgeous. And I soon discovered, at my niece's wedding, that we had more in common than just our passion for good underwear.

One of my sister Helen's daughters, Anne, married a lovely man called Neil Haftel, a scrap metal merchant. I was very surprised when Dawn arrived for the service and even more so when I saw she was accompanied by a very tall, handsome, black man.

It turned out that Lenny Henry and Neil had known each other for years and were good friends. It was lovely because, from then on, Dawn and I also had Neil and Anne to talk about whenever she came into the shop. When Lenny and Dawn were getting married they invited Anne and Neil to their wedding but on the Thursday before the ceremony Anne was rushed into hospital with a brain tumour. By the time Lenny and Dawn returned from their honeymoon three weeks later, Neil was a widower. My lovely niece died when she was only twenty-seven. It was very, very sad.

I used to see Lenny at the Bimal gym and he was always keen that Harold and I should keep in touch with Neil because, as Lenny put it, 'he is family'. Lenny was right, of course, but Neil had been married to Anne for such a short time and was only twenty-nine when she died. I felt we could only be a reminder of tragic times and when Neil remarried we thought it best to leave him to enjoy his new life.

And our own life was increasingly busy. We always knew we wanted to leave South Molton Street and four years later, when we were sure that our customers would be happy with the move, we transferred everything to Knightsbridge. We replaced the Contour fascia outside the shop with one that said Rigby & Peller. We could not believe what happened next.

Business went dead.

We had spent five years building up the Contour name and most people had never heard of Rigby & Peller: our customers thought we had vanished overnight. The minute we realised the problem, we quickly changed the fascia again. This time it said, 'Rigby & Peller, incorporating Contour'. We were very, very relieved when trade returned.

One aspect of the business that picked up quickly was the demand for maternity bras. When we first noticed (in our early Contour days) that we were being asked for nursing bras on a regular basis we started to ask the women in question why they had chosen to come to us. The answer was nearly always 'Betty Parsons'.

I did not know, never having been pregnant, who Betty Parsons was, but I made a point of finding out. It is impossible to explain to anyone who did not know Betty just how special she was. I have never known anyone like her and consider it a huge privilege to have been able to call her a friend.

Betty (her real name was Aileen but she hated it) had trained as a nurse, wanted to be an opera singer and found fame as a childbirth relaxation guru. Her mantra was, 'Drop your shoulders and relax'. It was a mantra that Betty shared with the mothers-to-be who attended classes at her Mayfair studio and with the Queen and various other royal ladies whom she had been called upon to help during their pregnancies. (It was also the first thing she ever used to say to me whenever we met up!)

Betty was a very practical and sympathetic woman. Over the years she helped thousands of women overcome their fear of childbirth and taught them different ways of controlling pain. She was not against drugs or hospitals at all – she believed in choice – but she had an unshakeable trust in the power of the mind.

One of my favourite stories about Betty was repeated in the obituary that the *Daily Telegraph* printed after her death in 2012. It had been suggested to Betty that another birthing expert had compared childbirth to orgasm. Betty's response? 'Well, honeys, if that's an orgasm, then keep me out of bed.'

Betty and I became very close friends and she was wonderful for me personally and also for business. We became the first port of call for Betty's 'girls', as she called them, when they needed maternity and nursing bras, and many continued to be regular customers. Even after Betty retired she would always be on the end of the phone to anyone who wanted advice, and was completely amazing. She and I would meet for lunch regularly and I enjoyed her company enormously. Betty lived until she was ninety-six but I wanted her to go on forever and miss her still.

There are many, many other famous people who are just regular customers and we have never felt the need to treat them differently to anyone else who walks through our door. The actress Joan Collins, on the other hand, always made me smile. She would come into the shop and stand by the door as if to say, 'I'm here!' – and if you didn't recognise her, God help you!

Inevitably, the Royal Warrant attracts business of a certain kind, but I have always maintained that it has never sold a bra. It is a wonderful recognition to have, but Harold has always considered it a double-edged sword. A Royal Warrant has credibility; it has history; it implies trustworthiness and reliability; and we are very lucky to have one. Conversely, some people look at it and only see pound signs, so it can put off potential customers. Everyone knows, for example that Rolls-Royce is a Royal Warrant holder but that doesn't mean everyone thinks, 'Oh yes, that's the car for me too'.

One of the hardest things we have had to overcome is that we are not as expensive as people think. For us, it is all about value and comfort. Most women think twice about spending, say, seventy-five pounds on a bra, but once you have one on, you immediately understand and can feel the difference.

Someone who understood this right away is the wonderful comedian Jo Brand. Jo first came into Rigby & Peller with Trinny Woodall and Susannah Constantine to film an episode for their hugely successful television series, *What Not to Wear*. Jo definitely needed help but was not a hundred per cent convinced that was possible. She said she struggled to find a bra to fit, let alone one that was comfortable. A short spell in the fitting room changed all that – of course it did. Jo said that she felt completely 'rejuvenated' in her new bra and it turned out that she was not just spinning a line for the camera. She was so thrilled that she came back and bought two thousand pounds' worth of gift vouchers so her friends and family could enjoy the same experience! How amazing is that?

Jo really is an extraordinary woman – funny, generous, highly intelligent and very sympathetic. I love her and I love the fact that she understood so quickly that the best gift you can give a woman – any woman – is a lingerie gift voucher (preferably a Rigby & Peller gift voucher, of course). Most people have no idea what to buy their mothers, daughters, sister or whoever, and what could be simpler than a gift voucher? And for the recipient it is perfect too. You are given a voucher so you make a day of it. You set off, enjoy a great shopping experience (made all the more so because you are not paying) and then you can go out and have a lovely lunch afterwards. That, to me, is not only the perfect present but the perfect day out. What is more, Harold was always equally enthusiastic about promoting gift vouchers as the ideal present, so there were never any arguments on that score.

One of the other things that never generated any debates is our membership of the Royal Warrant Holders' Association: the organisation that represents the companies and individuals who provide goods and services to Her Majesty the Queen, His Royal Highness the Duke of Edinburgh, or His Royal Highness the Prince of Wales.

There are about 800 members of the association and there are any number of interesting and entertaining social and networking events. One of David's favourite stories relates to the day he joined us for a garden party at Buckingham Palace. Everyone had badges with their company name on and Harold was talking to the Managing Director of Atco Lawn Mowers. 'Forgive me,' the man said (I can't remember his name), 'Rigby & Peller rings a bell but I cannot place what you do.'

Harold thought for a second and said, 'You could say we live off the fat of the land.'

It makes me laugh now but at the time I was definitely not impressed. (Mind you, I don't know why I was worried. The man did not know we were in the bra business and how likely is it that he would have realised – even if he had known – that Harold was referring to the fact that a large proportion of breast tissue is fat?) I nudged Harold, at which he immediately started talking about the problems he was having with the clutch cable on our Atco lawn mower! And this to the Managing Director, who had probably never got his hands dirty in all of his life.

It must have been around the same time that we decided that we had established the name of Rigby & Peller enough to be able to lose the Contour name altogether. We renamed the shop in the Whitgift Centre and decided that we would also benefit from having our own label. All our made-to-measure items carried a Rigby & Peller label but we were predominantly a business that sold up-market lingerie brands – products made by other people. We came to the conclusion that our own Rigby & Peller ready-to-wear range would be just the thing.

Harold did the homework and decided that a Finnish company met all our requirements. So, in 1988, Rigby & Peller took on an international dimension and our world changed in more ways than one.

CHAPTER SEVEN

Patricia of Finland made beautiful lingerie, but what was also important to us was that it was a family-owned firm with very similar values to our own. We had sold masses of Patricia bras over the years and when Harold was looking for a manufacturer to take on the Rigby & Peller brand, Patricia was an obvious contender.

The agreement was straightforward. We established a licensing agreement with the company that allowed them to put Rigby & Peller labels on some of their products which they could then sell to their existing customers, including us. We had prior approval, of course, on the ranges, styles and colours and had an input into the designs, but the products belonged to Patricia of Finland.

I cannot remember exactly, but I am sure the agreement would have specified our target market. In return we received a percentage of the sale of each and every product. What some people could not understand was that, even though the lingerie had our name on it, we had to buy the product like anyone else. Theoretically, just because we were Rigby & Peller, that did not give us preferential treatment but, obviously, Patricia would do us a favour if we needed it. We were by far and away their biggest customer in the UK so if we ever ran short of a particular Rigby & Peller item that a smaller customer had ordered, we would get the product first because they knew that we would sell it.

We launched the Rigby & Peller ready-to-wear collection at an invitation-only event at Fortnum & Mason and the reception was fantastic. It was a wonderful occasion, and for Harold and me almost surreal. We had never imagined that we would take the business to the heights that we had, but here we were with our very own brand and we were telling the world about it at one of the poshest shops in London. We also got lots of press coverage. Some of the photos taken in Hyde Park of our models, in big hats and nothing much else except our fabulous underwear, appeared all over the place. David was our official photographer on the day – a hard job for him, but someone had to do it!

1988 is also a memorable year thanks to our darling daughter Jill. When she had finished at Carmel College, Jill had gone to drama school in Hammersmith, but soon decided that what she really wanted to do was go to America. The first we heard of her ambition was when she came home and announced she had bought a one-way ticket to New York and asked me to drive her to the airport! It was absurd. She thought that the ten pounds she had in her pocket would see her through when she got there.

We thought differently.

We did not object to Jill going to New York but we wanted to know she would be safe. A friend arranged a refund on the ticket Jill had bought and we started all over again. Both our children were steeped in lingerie (figuratively speaking!) and Jill had helped in the shop since she was old enough to sort out stock. Eventually she became a Saturday junior and was popular with customers and staff alike.

We had recently started selling the Rigby & Peller range through various 'upscale' (as they call it) stores in America and the contacts we had made proved very useful. I made a couple of phone calls and arranged for Jill to work in the lingerie department of Henri Bendel, a chic women's wear shop on Fifth Avenue, until she found her feet. (We thought it would take her six months to sort out Henri Bendel's lingerie department but she did it in a morning!)

We went over with Jill to settle her into New York and found her a room at the 92nd Street Y, the Jewish equivalent of the YMCA. I can remember leaving her when we had to return to England and both Harold and I were very wobbly. Harold has never been a kissy-huggy sort of man but he adores the children and felt as anxious as I did leaving our girl behind.

We felt even more anxious when Jill managed to get kicked out of the 92nd Street Y for smuggling a friend in to stay the night in her room. I got a phone call in London telling me that Jill had to leave immediately as the 'no visitors' rule was inviolable. I was indignant, but the woman would not be moved and Jill had to look for somewhere else there and then. She found a place off 42nd Street, which turned out to be a favoured haunt of hookers, but Jill didn't mind. Her rented apartment came with complimentary cockroaches and rats (it was above a Chinese restaurant) but even that did not faze our Jill. Harold and I were so horrified when we saw it that we ended up buying an apartment in Greenwich Village. It was a sweet little place that became Jill's home for the eight years she stayed in New York, and doubled as Rigby & Peller's American office.

It was wonderful for us having Jill in America because she could go and do fitting sessions in the stores that sold Rigby & Peller and was on hand if any problems arose. She has a wonderful way with customers and everybody loves her. Harold and I used to go over two or three times a year and Jill always joined us on the promotional tours. We had some amazing adventures.

I have always said that the Royal Warrant does not sell bras, but in terms of promotion in America it was huge. Every store we went into would make a big thing of the fact that I was the royal corsetiere and often they would offer fittings complete with afternoon tea! They would set up occasional tables with crisp, starched cloths and use the prettiest tea sets to serve scones with jam and cream – all in the middle of a lingerie department. They thought it was very British; we thought it was very funny. What was not funny was the size of some of the women we were asked to fit. I have never seen so many huge people. We offered a good range of sizes in Rigby & Peller but things got difficult when a woman needed a cup size between J and N. In such instances we would have to go out into the store and search the other brands to see if we could find something that would fit.

I loved doing the sales tours with Jill but I never enjoyed Los Angeles because the customers were very difficult. I'll never forget one woman who came in for a fitting and drove me bonkers. I must have tried dozens and dozens of bras on her and I breathed a sigh a relief when she finally decided there was one she liked. 'The thing is,' she drawled, 'it's just soooo expensive.' The gorgeous confection of a bra was thirty-five dollars.

Without a word of thanks the woman sailed out of the fitting room and plonked herself at the table to enjoy a cream tea. I could not get over it and she must have caught my expression because she turned on me. 'Am I not supposed to be having scones?' she asked in a loud, cutting voice. All I could do was smile because if I had opened my mouth I would have let her have a piece of my mind!

The customers back in England were much easier to please, and our own brand was doing very nicely alongside the other labels that we sold. We were often asked for samples for fashion shows and magazine shoots and we never turned down the opportunity. Rigby & Peller became very well known and I enjoyed being the person journalists called on when they wanted a comment or wanted to write an article on some aspect or other of lingerie.

Looking back over years and years of press articles it is surprising how often I was called on to say the same thing: eighty-five per cent of women are wearing the wrong size bra. You would be amazed at how many women are walking around in a B and they are really an E or F. So many women simply do not understand the importance of fitting.

Years ago it was commonplace to get fitted for bras but then Marks & Spencer and other high street chains decided they were going to offer acres and acres of bras and let women help themselves. Why bother paying for fitters when customers can see for themselves what they like and can try it on by themselves if they want? The problem is that most women haven't got a clue. They end up buying the best of a selection that they should never have made in the first place. So many women I have met admit to having a drawer full of ill-fitting or downright uncomfortable bras which they never even bothered to try on before they bought them.

I really cannot grasp why English women are resistant to the benefits of good underwear. Years ago I used to go to the first day of Harrods sale and I always went to where they were selling the designer wear because that was a real eye-opener. Harrods used to put up a temporary communal fitting room where you could go in and try on anything you liked. It was a mess. There would be women putting on the most beautiful clothes over the most disgusting underwear. (In that changing room you could be excused for thinking that grey was the in colour for bras because there were so many tatty once-white disasters!)

The right underwear makes your clothes look better. Good foundations are the key to good grooming. I do not understand why generation upon generation of women refuse to learn what is, after all, a simple lesson: never buy a bra without being correctly fitted by a good bra-fitter. End of lesson.

Someone who understood the lesson so well that she liked to wear her underwear on the outside, was the wonderfully eccentric and aristocratic fashionista, Isabella Blow. At various times Isabella worked for *Tatler*, *Vogue* and the *Sunday Times* and was famous for being a brilliant talent-spotter. Her best friend was the milliner, Philp Treacy (whom she discovered) and she would come into the shop wearing totally over-the-top hats. (Mrs Blow always wore something on her head; even if it was a bird's nest.)

In Isabella Blow I found a customer for the original Rigby & Peller treasures that I had stored in silk-lined suitcases several years before. She was fun to serve. She had a terrific figure and the more outrageous a corset or basque, the more she loved it. Several Rigby & Peller pieces featured in an exhibition Isabella staged at the Victoria & Albert Museum and were also used for one of her gorgeous coffee-table books. Tragically, Isabella Blow committed suicide when she was only forty-eight years old by drinking weed-killer. It was terrible. There were lots of tributes to her in the papers and one of my favourites was in the *Guardian*. One of her friends, Geordie Greig, wrote in her obituary that Isabella Blow (or Issie as she was known) was 'the friendliest, most generous, exciting, impossible, inventive, life-enhancing wonderful woman in fashion'. Certainly, I have never had a customer like her.

One of the other fun commissions we had was to make monster bras for *The Benny Hill Show* and *The Two Ronnies*. I never met the three gentlemen in person because all our dealings were with the wardrobe department, but it was fun seeing our creations on screen.

The men who genuinely wanted lingerie for themselves, we served after-hours. There were several transvestites who enjoyed the luxury of Rigby & Peller and we were happy to oblige them as long as we could do so without upsetting any of our regular customers.

In 1990 David came to the decision that he did not want to work with cars, he just wanted to own them. Our wonderful son was unsure what to do to earn the money he needed to indulge his passion so he came to join us at Rigby & Peller until he could make up his mind. Luckily for us, David decided the lingerie business suited him well. It was amazing. He was another Harold and slotted into the business with no trouble at all. Mind you, David had form. When he was at Carmel College, he used to pounce on the lingerie posters we were always being sent so he could take them to school to sell them. It turned out there was quite a market for pictures of scantily clad young women!

One of the first new products that David was involved with was what we called a 'slimslip'. Today there is a huge range of control garments but in those days the choice was limited. Our slimslip was effectively a control petticoat that incorporated a pair of knickers. It smoothed your thighs down and kept your tummy in. Perfect.

In 1991 Madonna caused a fuss at the Cannes Film Festival by not wearing a gorgeous evening dress but taking to the red carpet in only a satin bra (with ridiculous pointed cups) and a matching girdle. There were pictures of Madonna in that outfit everywhere and the *Sun* approached us to ask us to make a replica so they could offer it as a reader prize. We were very happy to oblige – and also made sure that the story mentioned that a Rigby & Peller slimslip was just as effective as a Madonna girdle and substantially cheaper!

The slimslip became a popular product and we sold lots of them through our own shops as well as other up-market outlets. One of the other things we came up with was something we called 'converti' straps. In those days, if you wanted to wear a dress that was backless, or just cut low at the back, you had to buy a special bra. I came to the conclusion that that was unnecessary when you could adapt a bra you already owned. We designed and had made long straps that hooked onto the hooks and eyes on a bra strap and then, once crossed over, wrapped around your waist and clipped closed at the front, pulling the whole back of the bra down at the same time. It was very simple but hugely effective. We sold loads of them at our own shops and through other retailers as well.

Harold and David looked after the finance of the project and I did the promotion. It worked very well. People sometimes used to ask how my men coped being surrounded by models prancing around in next to nothing, but it never worried them at all. Both of them just took it in their stride.

Our next major decision was to switch manufacturers for our own Rigby & Peller brand. We had had a good working relationship with Patricia of Finland but, inevitably, distance became an issue. Helsinki is a long way to go for design meetings and we finally decided that, because all our products had the Royal Warrant on the label, it would be much better if we found a British manufacturer. On top of that our market base was mainly in the UK and the styles of bra that sell well here are not always popular overseas.

We did lots of homework and ended up joining forces with a company called Fantasie, which was a brand owned by a group called Stirling Brands, based in Kettering in Northamptonshire: Stirling Brands was one of the biggest textile manufacturers of the day in the UK. Fantasie was quite small at that stage but they made the style and quality of products we wanted – their bras were gorgeous – and they were looking for an up-market brand to add to their stable. Fantasie set up a Rigby & Peller team who became our main point of contact and we established the same sort of licensing agreement we had had with Patricia of Finland. Several years later, there was a management buyout at Stirling Brands but we continued working with the successor company, Evedon, until the time came when we decided to go it alone.

Our requirements were quite specific but the number of items we needed was relatively small. It became clear that it would be much better for us to have total control of our own brand so we quietly worked away in the background looking at alternatives. The most important thing was to make sure that there would be no gap in supply when we switched our manufacturing base.

Eventually we realised that to retain the quality we needed, yet remain competitive, the only viable option for us was to turn to the Far East. David and Harold took charge of making all the necessary arrangements and, as always, kept a tight rein on the finances when we commissioned a Chinese manufacturer. Our Head of Buying at the time, and her assistant, were in charge of design but (as you can imagine) I had an input, along with all the other female members of the team.

It was all very exciting because the choice was wonderful. When we started out selling lingerie, bras were either white or black; now the fabrics are mind-blowingly fantastic and there is a gorgeous array of colours. I was, it must be said, a little like a child in a sweetie shop but Harold kept me in check (well, most of the time). He and David ran the Rigby & Peller 'engine room' and decided whether we could afford my ideas or not! My Harold's guiding principle is to never be beholden to a bank and we financed all our ventures ourselves for many a year.

Alongside Rigby & Peller ready-to-wear, the bespoke business was ticking along nicely. It received an extra boost when the 'golden boy' of British design at the time, John Galliano, asked if we could help him. John wanted various ready-to-wear items and about twenty-five girdles and bras made especially to his design for his spring show in Paris. His team sent through the list and the instructions and the girls in the work room put in lots of extra hours to meet the deadline. I only met John once but was very touched that, when he could not make our final meeting, he sent me a lovely note written below one of his original sketches. (It now hangs, framed, in our hall.)

Harold and I went to the Paris show, which was wonderful, although we were a little disappointed that Rigby & Peller was not mentioned in the programme. We were even more disappointed three months later when our bill for £3,037.96 was still outstanding.

I believe that problems arose when John's relationship with his backer, Peder Bertelsen, went sour. Mr Bertelsen, originally a Danish oil and property tycoon, had become the biggest designer retailer in London via his company Aguecheek Limited. The company had been very supportive of John but it was reported in the *Mail on Sunday* that the Galliano show had lost Peder Bertelsen a million pounds.

If that is true, our debt, in comparison, was tiny, but we tried all the normal 'gentlemanly' routes to solve the problem. When nothing was forthcoming a little press release was sent out saying we were considering putting the matter in the hands of a debt collector, which is not our preferred style and not a route we take lightly. In the end, that is what we had to do and it did result in everything being settled amicably.

Like any business we were not complete strangers to bad debt. We used to run a system whereby if you wanted to buy a bra or corset to wear under a particular outfit you could take it home, 'on appro', and try it on. The girls in the shop would take down the customer's credit card details as a guarantee. If the customer was happy we would charge her credit card, or she could return the item without charge. End of story. Unfortunately, over a period of time we ended up with a number of bad debts so we had to limit the system to customers we knew well.

One customer I came to know and love was the Queen Mother. I had been invited to attend Her Royal Highness several years after I started serving her daughters and while I was nervous, I was also excited.

Clarence House was quite old-fashioned but in the hall was the wonderful portrait of the Queen Mother and her daughters taken by Norman Parkinson in 1980 – the one in which the three of them are wearing blue satin cloaks. The portrait was huge but really beautiful and you only need to see it once (there is a print in the National Portrait Gallery) to understand why Norman Parkinson is considered one of the best portrait photographers of the twentieth century.

The Queen Mother was great fun and lovely to serve. Once I dared to comment on an outfit she had worn recently. 'You look wonderful in lilac, Ma'am,' I said.

'It was rather nice wasn't it? But I prefer myself in blue. When I am in blue, and waving in the back of a car, people can see me so much better.'

I was with the Queen Mother once when she was told that her hat-maker had arrived and Princess Margaret was on her way. Mother and daughter shared the same milliner and the Queen Mother laughed when she told me that the Princess liked to interfere. 'Shall I tell you what I do?' Her Royal Highness said.

As you can imagine, I was all ears.

'I pretend to listen to Margaret and then, once she has gone, I order exactly what I want.' As always, there was a twinkle in her eye.

I was granted the Royal Warrant to the Queen Mother in 1993. It was a fantastic year for Rigby & Peller, not only because of royalty but also thanks to a young Australian with a nose for a good story.

CHAPTER EIGHT

A year earlier, a pretty young woman, Madonna Benjamin, came to see us to ask if we could help her. Madonna, previously a journalist with *Vogue*, was working for Fulmar Television and Film as a researcher/assistant producer but she wanted to become a director. She had applied for a place on a BBC scheme that involved her having to submit a ten-minute film. She wanted to make it on Rigby & Peller because, she said, 'this place is just like a little drama in itself, with all these wonderful women who are ready-made characters'.

Put like that, how could we refuse?

Timing was important too. There were to be several television programmes in 1993 to celebrate the fortieth anniversary of the Queen's coronation and Madonna had the clever idea that a film on the Queen's corsetieres might be something different.

Madonna made a terrific ten-minute film that got her onto the shortlist but, sadly, not a place on the '10 x 10' initiative being run by the Bristol-based BBC Documentary Department. Not to be deterred, she sent a proposal to Carlton Television, the company that was due to take over from Thames Television as the main independent television station. The biggest of the Carlton bigwigs was not immediately smitten but Madonna's proposal was picked up from his in-tray by someone else in the department who fell in love with the idea. The outcome was that, instead of just buying her short film, they asked Madonna to make a full half-hour documentary on Rigby & Peller. It was the first documentary that Carlton commissioned for its Tuesday peak-time slot and everyone was very excited.

Madonna wrote to tell us that she had been given the go-ahead and I remember Harold and I being stunned when we read that the programme might attract 'many millions' of viewers. Many millions! We knew that the filming would be disruptive but who could turn down such a golden opportunity? Certainly, not us.

Madonna was very organised and we received a detailed shooting schedule telling us which members of staff would be involved on what days and what we should expect. The plan was to do all the filming over six days but I think, in the end, it took closer to three weeks! In light of what we do, Fulmar thoughtfully put together an all-women film crew and they were fabulous. Madonna was the producer/director; there was a camera woman and sound woman, and a broadcast journalist called Sue Margolis, who often worked for *Woman's Hour*, did the interviewing and wrote the script.

My biggest concern was that one of the staff would say something out of order and every morning I warned them to bite their tongues and watch what they said. 'The fact that Madonna is my best friend at the moment means nothing. If you say anything scandalous she will use it.' And, of course, she did.

The manager of the Knightsbridge shop at the time didn't pay any attention to what I said. I wanted to take her out and sack her on the spot when she moaned on camera about women who spend their whole time shopping. 'Some of the customers who you know are just shoppers and have nothing else to do all day long… I wish they would do some charity work and do something with themselves and not just shop every single day. You think there must be more to life than this shopping but for them that is their life.' I was furious. Get rid of women who like shopping! Who did she think paid her wages? I was very glad when that particular manager finally left us.

Then one of our lovely long-time members of staff, Helen, explained that no one was allowed to see the delights that went to Buckingham Palace but that she had once seen 'a bikini of Princess Margaret's'. I have no idea what bikini Helen was talking about, but it certainly was not Princess Margaret's – Her Royal Highness only ever wore one-piece swimsuits. (Although some of them were made of two pieces that linked together, they were nothing like a bikini.)

And then there was (and still is) the seamstress who makes everything for the Queen. When Sue Margolis asked her what she thought of the monarchy, she said she thought 'they should have their heads chopped off because they're a waste of money'! I have to add that that particular seamstress is French and has always been a little cantankerous, but she nearly had a breakdown when she saw that they had left her comment in the final film. I was livid, but what could I do?

I did not have any concerns about our customers who featured in the film – they were amazing. Emma Macpherson, who looked rather vampish, flashed a little of her favourite scarlet bra as she praised the virtues of her Rigby & Peller purchases in helping 'snare' boyfriends; and there was Carolyn Stratton, who considered herself something of a socialite. Mrs Stratton appeared for the filming in fuchsia pink silk from head to toe, complete with an enormous frilly pink hat. No matter that she looked more like she was going to Ascot rather than a bra-fitting, Mrs Stratton gushed and gooed and said how wonderful Rigby & Peller was at giving her a cleavage, so that was all good.

Our 'random' shopper was a young, big-busted woman from Balham whom Madonna knew. Brenda Gilhooley had never had a fitting before and brought in a bag full of bras that she couldn't wear. She tipped them all over the counter before I shoved them all back and marched her into the fitting room. I admit that I made a bit of a 'matzoh pudding' of the fitting for the benefit of the camera. I tried Brenda in far more bras than I really needed to, but I wanted to stress how important it is to try a bra on. Even if you think you know what size you are (and I doubt it) every single style of bra is different, so you have to try them on. (I know, I have said it before and you can be sure that I will probably say it again.)

The customer who stole the show, though, was an international city banker called Selina Elwell, who had been loyal to Rigby & Peller for years. Her passion for us aside, Mrs Elwell's greatest attraction, as far as Madonna was concerned, was that she had a very posh accent and cut-glass vowels. Early on in the documentary Mrs Elwell explained that she had been coming to Rigby & Peller for years not only because of 'the misery of mass-produced bras' but that she had always been, 'something of a reactionary. At a time when other people were burning their bras, I was having mine made-to-measure at Rigby & Peller.' It was wonderful.

It also fell to Selina Elwell to have the last word when talking about Rigby & Peller. 'It's not,' pronounced Mrs Elwell, 'about the rich or the famous. It's about ordinary people, like one.' You couldn't have made it up!

Madonna called the documentary *Giving the Empire a Lift*, which we thought was brilliant, and it was scheduled to go out on Tuesday 1 June 1993. We decided we should be prepared. Even if Carlton was way over the mark on its audience estimate, we thought we might get a few more people popping into the shop to have a look.

I decided that it would not hurt to overplay it. I put out a press release beforehand saying that we were concerned about the potential rush of customers and did not want to upset Mr Al Fayed (who by then owned Harrods) by having a crush of people on Hans Road. Accordingly, I said, Rigby & Peller were employing a commissionaire to deal with the crowds. It was rubbish really, just a public relations stunt, but I did ring the Corps of Commissionaires and ask if a woman commissionaire could be with us on Wednesday 2 June. I envisaged she would be there for a day or two and that would be that.

The next morning I arrived at the shop to discover a smart, uniformed commissionaire standing outside the door. 'Oh my God, you're not a woman!'

'No, I never have been,' smiled the man, who introduced himself as Ted Chinner.

I immediately rang the Corps of Commissionaires and explained that Rigby & Peller is a ladies' lingerie shop and that we needed a doorwoman, not a doorman. The person on the other end of the phone was very understanding and apologetic but explained that Ted was the only person free to take on the job. 'Well, I suppose he can stay for today,' I said.

How wrong was I!

Ted was with us for more than ten years and I was distraught when he finally left us through ill-health. Ted loved Rigby & Peller and, in turn, was loved by all of us and all our customers. He would open the door for people, even if they weren't planning to come to the shop; he would look after dogs, hail taxis, help people across the road – he was the most amazing man ever.

Ted showed his worth from that very first day. We were over-run with customers and had to rush out and buy some cloakroom tickets so we could have an orderly queue rather than a rabble. Ted gave out the tickets to people as they arrived and explained how long they would have to wait for a fitting. He arranged that they could go to the Italian restaurant next door for coffee (courtesy of Rigby & Peller) or go to Harrods and come back later. He was magic at sorting everybody out. Meanwhile, inside the shop, the girls were working as quickly as they could and Gerda and I dealt with the phones.

The most extraordinary thing was that most of the calls were from men wanting to make an appointment for their wives. I suddenly realised that every man thinks his wife is the only woman who does not know what bra to buy. She complains, but he doesn't go round the golf course asking his friends if their wives have to take their bras off in the evening because they are so uncomfortable; he doesn't sit at the bridge table and say, 'My wife has such a problem with bras, does yours?' Of course he doesn't. Millions of men who watched *Giving the Empire a Lift* suddenly realised the truth of the matter and thousands of them reached for the phone.

We thought the rush would slow down after a few days, but nothing could have been further from the truth. We had to buy a ticket machine – a smart version of the ones they have on cheese counters – to give Ted a break. It became quite normal on a Saturday for the wait for a fitting to be two to three hours. It was madness. Our footfall increased by a hundred per cent and the sales figures went up by something like sixty-five per cent. So much for the recession!

We were still trying to catch our breath when the follow-ing month David married his long-term girlfriend, Simona Beerman, a legal secretary. Simona's mother is Italian and her father (who died in 2006) was English and much to our delight she was not only gorgeous, she was Jewish (and still is both!). I would be lying if I said it did not matter.

I will never forget how upset my parents were, years ago, when my brother, Lewis, announced he was going to marry his non-Jewish girlfriend, Joyce. (I would never have dared bring home a boy who was not Jewish!) Joyce happily converted to Judaism and came to live with us to learn the Jewish ways before she and Lewis got married; but as far as my parents were concerned you were either born Jewish or you were not. (The whole thing about Jewishness being passed from mother to child is complicated, but the general rule is that if your mother is Jewish, you are Jewish; if your father is Jewish but your mother is not, then you are not Jewish.) But I thought Joyce was a wonderful person and I loved her very much.

It was Lewis and Joyce who often used to swoop me up at weekends when I was at Lillesden. Lewis would pick me up from school and take me back to Brighton where Joyce would feed me about four different meals before Lewis took me back. I tried to tell her that the food at school was very good but she never believed me and worried that I was not getting enough! It was very sad that they did not have children but Joyce became a huge part of our family and I was desperately sad when Lewis divorced her after twenty-five years of marriage. (Ironically, the divorce would have upset my parents even more than Lewis marrying Joyce in the first place!)

David and Simona's wedding, on Sunday 4 July 1993 (David calls it his 'Loss of Independence Day') was a very happy occasion. Jill came home from New York to be Maid of Honour, which made it even more special for us.

Carlton screened *Giving the Empire a Lift* again in August; it featured on in-flight entertainment lists; most of the regional networks bought it and lots of overseas stations snatched it up too. I only learned this because several months later I received a lovely card from a woman in a tiny town in New Zealand addressed to me and all the staff.

> Dear All,
>
> I so enjoyed *Giving the Empire a Lift* that I wished I could visit your establishment to be fitted by your competent 'London's best known corsetiere'.
>
> Every little problem which you pointed out to your full-busted customer, I have experienced over the years.
>
> I am a 76-year-old person – 5 feet 2 inches in height, weighing 8 stone 4lbs and I wear 34 inch <u>DD</u> bras, so you can imagine I carry an ample bosom in front of me.
>
> I know you said goodbye to a very satisfied lady!
>
> I thought the programme was extremely interesting and I was sorry when it ended. I appreciated all the comments – I just had to write to you.
>
> Marjorie M. Suckling

How wonderful is that? I don't think there has ever been a programme before or since that took you inside a fitting room, so it was obviously very special.

Marjorie Suckling's letter was addressed to me at Rigby & Peller, Knightsbridge, London, UK – no street address or postcode. (Isn't our postal service marvellous?) I kept it, not only because it came from so far away and was so sweet, but because Marjorie Suckling and I had quite a lot in common in terms of measurements in those days – with the exception of the double D cup!

One of the other amazing off-shoots of the programme was that it was not only Rigby & Peller who benefited. The *Drapers Record* later that year reported that several lingerie specialists around the country had seen the demand for bra fittings go up and sales increase accordingly since the programme had been aired. It was also around the same time that Marks & Spencer, I believe, decided to introduce a bra-fitting service. (I cannot swear that was because of Madonna's brilliant documentary, but you never know.)

What I do know is that business for Rigby & Peller did not calm down and I was in demand for more and more television interviews, including one for an Australian channel. The endless interest confirmed for me what I always knew: when I talk about bras – and I talk about bras a lot – I am talking to half the population of the world. (Not quite half actually, because there are slightly more boys born than girls, but the difference is tiddly and girls live longer.) Every woman is different but every woman has two things in common with every other. The need to be well supported is universal and television companies could not get enough of me saying exactly that. It was wonderful.

One of the things that the television interviewers loved was my ceremonial 'throwing away' bin. We got into the habit of inviting customers to leave their ill-fitting bra behind once we had fitted them properly. Often a woman would say, 'No, I'll wear it when I'm gardening or walking the dog.' My standard reply was, 'I don't think so,' as I lifted the bin up, but what really changed people's minds was when I told them that their cast-offs were needed by others.

There was a big campaign, initiated by the Salvation Army in Kettering, where there was a central clothing bank, to collect items for homeless people and those in the third world. We decided it would be great to collect underwear to add to the collection. Nobody had done that before and it was hugely successful. It was so successful that underwear became a necessary item in all clothing packages sent to Africa. I was told that it got to the stage that unless four per cent of every consignment was underwear, it would be snubbed. The campaign really caught the imagination of our customers and we ended up sending hundreds and hundreds of bras to the Salvation Army.

We put out a press release saying that Rigby & Peller was happy to receive cast-offs from anyone who wanted to help the campaign and, once again, the footfall in the shop soared. We decided that we needed to reconfigure the shop to make it easier to cope with the increased flow of customers – but we did not want to stop trading. The answer proved very simple.

We took a short-term rent on premises round the corner in Brompton Road and hired a man with a van to move everything out of one shop into the other. On the day of the move there was a bit of a hiccup. A few of the crates that were full of bras fell out and crashed onto the road. At the time Capital Radio had what they called 'The Flying Eye', a helicopter patrol of London to report on traffic problems. You can imagine how much we laughed when we heard Russ Kane on the radio inform the listeners that there was a problem in Knightsbridge. 'One lane on Brompton Road,' he said, 'is blocked by a bra spillage.' It was as absurd as it sounds.

We were in our temporary shop for about six weeks and, while we were there, Ted stood outside the Hans Road shop and directed customers round the corner. It all worked perfectly, but once we were back on home ground it got so busy again that Harold decided we had to have another shop.

He finally settled on one he found in Mayfair. (We had closed the shop in the Whitgift Centre a few years earlier, when the lease came up for renewal, because we wanted to concentrate on Knightsbridge.)

I was worried because Conduit Street was dead. It seemed to me to be just a row of boring old airline offices: Harold thought that it had potential because of its location. Harold won. We leased a shop that had two floors, which gave us much-needed storage space, but the best thing of all was that the rent was far from extravagant.

With suitable fanfare and a champagne reception, Rigby & Peller Mayfair opened in 1995. And no sooner had we opened the doors than we had to install a ticket machine there too to cope with the queues. It was only then, I think, that Harold and I fully appreciated the amazing power of all the publicity we had received.

Taking a fall for the Women's Campaign for Soviet Jewry at the Streatham Ice Rink in October 1973. (© Alpha Press)

Marking the day Sylva Zalmanson was freed. L–R: John Moore MP, Me, Ruth Urban, Bernard Wetherill MP and Rita Horowitz. (Courtesy of the *Croydon Advertiser*)

The day twenty-two 35ers chained ourselves to the Foreign Office railings as part of our campaign to highlight the plight of Soviet Jewish Prisoners of Conscience. (©Alpha Press)

The silk negligee set we sent to Lady Diana Spencer on the announcement of her engagement to Prince Charles in February 1981.

The exterior of Rigby & Peller in South Moulton Street in 1982. (Courtesy of Ronald G. Smith)

The Royal Coat of Arms as displayed outside Rigby & Peller in Knightsbridge.

The exterior of Rigby & Peller in Hans Road in Knightsbridge, 1986 when we had to include the Contour name to revive business!

Opposite: Launch of our own Rigby & Peller range in 1988.

Harold and me at the launch of our own Rigby & Peller range. An exciting day.

Filming *Giving the Empire a Lift* in 1992 in the Knightsbridge store. L–R: The director, Madonna Benjamin; R&P customer, Carolyn Stratton; camerawoman, Cinders Forshaw.

One of the scenes in
Giving the Empire a Lift.

The one and only
Ted Chinner on
duty outside the
Knightsbridge store,
c. 1994.

Harold and me with our secretary, Gerda Oblath, en route to Buckingham Palace.

Rigby & Peller Mayfair in Conduit Street, 1995.

CHAPTER NINE

Over the years I had kept in touch with many of my special friends with whom I had shared so much in our campaign for Soviet Jewry, and in the early 1990s, Rita Eker, who had been co-chair of the 35s committee, came up with a new idea. She and a clever man, the social entrepreneur David Altschuler, realised that many of the families who had escaped Russia and set up home in Israel needed financial support. The One to One Project was born.

The project did all sorts of things, but the most challenging fund-raising idea was to get people to sign up for sponsored treks through the harsh landscape that our ancestors had experienced more than three thousand years before. You had to pay to go on a trek and were eligible to apply only if you raised a minimum of one thousand five hundred pounds in sponsorship – a daunting prospect in itself.

I read about the first trek, in 1994, and decided that I was going to do the next one. Everybody thought I was completely mad. Harold knew he would not be able to join me in slogging across the Sinai desert, or any desert come to that, because his feet are not strong enough; but he knew how determined I was and, as ever, was as supportive as he could be. I had a year to get really fit. And if I was going to get fit, Harold was too.

We had employed a personal trainer for several years, a lovely New Zealand girl called Sarah Prenter. Once a week we would clear the racks from the centre of the Knightsbridge shop and Sarah would give us a step aerobics session that any of the staff could join in. On another day she would come and put Harold and me through our paces at home. With Jill away in America, Sarah became a little like a surrogate daughter and she sometimes even shared Shabbat with us. We had a great relationship, which worked for her too because her family was so far away.

When I started having trouble with my back Sarah decided to take me to see her physiotherapist. I was horrified when she said he was in Chiswick, but Sarah insisted. How glad I am that she did.

Martin Haines worked in partnership with Alan Watson and together they ran the Bimal Medical and Sports Rehabilitation Clinic. They both lived in Nottingham and used to go home at weekends, but during the week they ran their very busy practice in London. They were wonderful. When Martin decided he wanted to stay in Nottingham with his family and not come to London anymore, I transferred to being Alan's patient. I love Martin (he still sends us a Christmas card every year) but Alan became my rock and a major part of my life. I cannot tell you how important he was to me.

When I told him about the trek I wanted to do, he decided I needed a more strenuous routine. By this stage Sarah had returned home to New Zealand so I was working with a lovely man called Steve Thomas. On Mondays Steve would come to us at home with his now-wife-then-girlfriend, Nicky, who was a masseuse; and on Wednesdays and Fridays I would meet Steve at the Bimal gym. We became very close. I like to be good friends with the people I spend time with – even if I am paying someone to be with me, I think of that person as a friend rather than an employee. It's just how I am. Steve and Nicky encouraged me tremendously and they were very much a part of my life. (We even went to their wedding in Wales when they finally tied the knot.) Steve was a wonderful trainer. He knew all my idiosyncrasies and knew how far to push me. We spent three hours a week together and I thought he was simply wonderful. I used to have to leave home in Croydon early in the morning to arrive in Chiswick for 8.30 a.m. but it was worth it. I would have a coffee and then I would work out for an hour and a half before having a shower, getting dressed and going to work. I found it really hard, but there was unexpected compensation.

It was at Bimal that I met Princess Diana. She would see Alan on a Friday morning and then her trainer would take her through a routine in the gym. It was only a small gym so, inevitably, there was a bit of breathless (on my part) banter and we got talking. After several months the Princess invited Harold and me to lunch at Kensington Palace and we got to know each other as friends. Whenever we went to the palace she would run down the stairs to meet us.

Diana was always very thoughtful. Once Jill came to lunch with me and the first course was fish. When my daughter explained that, unfortunately, she didn't eat fish, she was instantly told not to worry. Diana had a button under the table by her chair and two seconds later, Paul Burrell appeared with a new dish of something else for Jill. There was no fuss and no comment – that was so typical of Diana.

This was around the time when Diana was at odds with the Royal Family and I think she liked to have people around her who were removed from her rarefied world. Once, when she rang me (we spoke a lot on the phone), I had to race in from the garden. She made me tell her all about what I had been doing in great detail. On that occasion I had got my hands dirty putting in some bedding plants, but I had to be honest and confess that my idea of gardening is more about telling the gardener what to do rather than doing it myself! We often talked about the demands of juggling business and family and I think that she loved hearing about my everyday life because her life was a long way from conventional.

She knew what I did of course, and used to refer to Rigby & Peller as 'headquarters'. She would ring up and say, 'I'm coming to headquarters, will you be there?' Of course I was always there for Diana. She really was a genuinely warm person. It used to make me smile that I would have to go to 10 Downing Street for Cherie Blair, but Princess Diana would come to us because, I think, she enjoyed getting out and about.

We have a lovely photo on our wall of Princess Diana meeting the staff outside the shop in Hans Road and she is holding a big bunch of flowers. It was not a bouquet we had bought for her, but one she was bringing to me. She loved flowers and whenever you went to lunch at Kensington Palace there would always be a bunch on your chair. There would always be her butler, Paul Burrell, as well and we became quite friendly with him too. There wasn't anything he wouldn't do for Princess Diana and I liked him: there was no reason *not* to like Paul, he was just so affable.

I never met Diana's boys but I used to give her lingerie and swimwear posters for them to put up in their studies at Eton. She was always talking about her sons; they were always on her mind.

Diana really was very beautiful and had the most amazing figure. She was just right. We were talking once about swimwear and I asked if she wanted to see the new range from a company called Gottex (they make the most gorgeous things). The company was so excited that they arranged a private viewing and the company's owner, Mrs Gottlieb, flew over from Israel to greet the Princess personally. It was great fun and Leah Gottlieb thought Diana's visit was the best thing that had ever happened in her career! It was lovely for everyone. Diana ordered a few things and the company made a cover-up for her to match the swimwear of her choice, and a beach bag too. It was very successful. (All the swimwear that Diana wore on the yacht, during that last fateful holiday she shared with Dodi Fayed, was what she had chosen from the Gottex range on that magical day several months previously.)

The whole world has written about Princess Diana's death and I will not add anything. It was a terrible, terrible tragedy and I was heartbroken. The one consolation is that I had the great privilege of knowing her as a friend: I cherish my memories of her.

I did my first trek in November 1995 – one month short of my sixtieth birthday. I had to buy a sleeping bag, the first I had ever owned (I had never slept in a tent before, let alone on the ground) and all the necessary hiking gear – we had been warned it could be freezing at night so thermal socks and vests were high on the list. I rolled and scrunched everything into my new backpack and set off for what was to be the greatest adventure of my life.

I knew I was fit but I was still worried. Our trek was billed, 'From Mount Sinai to the Promised Land' and involved five days covering nearly 100 kilometres on foot across what I had been told was the uninviting, scary and challenging Sinai desert. Would I really be up to it? Harold was very encouraging and I treasure the letter that Alan Watson of Bimal sent me just before I was due to leave:

I thought that I would just place in writing the thoughts which I have regarding the Mount Sinai to The Promised Land walk which you are undertaking next week. It has been a profoundly sad time for the people of Israel over the last week in particular, with the tragic loss of a remarkable man and leader of your people [Yitzhak Rabin]. A man who had the visions and commitment to lead your promised land into a period of perceived peace and harmony between neighbouring states.

In each of you he has left a part of that desire to succeed and to commit something in return to your country. The words of President Kennedy, 'Ask not what I can take from my country but what I can give to my country and its people' [*sic*] is an honourable way to live one's life and you have shown qualities which endorse that philosophy.

I am so proud and honoured to know you as a person who has the strength and desire to put something back to life and who works to achieve and develop yourself in many ways.

The commitment which you have shown for this project has been tremendous and I have the utmost admiration for the way that you have remained focused on the goal whilst having to suffer physical pain and emotional stress along the long period of time which you have been working to achieve the necessary fitness over the last year.

A lesser person would have faltered and taken the easy route (has anybody got a bus?!). You have shown that spirit that exists in so many of your great people who have built your country into a land which will reach the promised land and will, without doubt, take you along from Mount Sinai to The Promised Land.

You must remember June that you are physically fit enough for this project, that you are strong enough and have the aerobic capability to reach your goal; and that with your will and desire, you will accomplish your targets…

All those wonderful, complimentary things made me cry, and I was hugely grateful that Alan went on to give me some very sensible advice about drinking lots of water and pacing myself. But the paragraph I clung to was the last one I have quoted.

It turned out that Alan was right.

There were about eighty of us booked on the trek and the first time we got together was at Gatwick for an early morning flight to Sharm El-Sheikh in Egypt. While I knew some people, everyone was so friendly that it was obvious immediately that I would be in good company. The excitement was huge and was only dented a little when, about an hour into the flight, the captain announced that for some reason or other most of our luggage was back at Gatwick. He assured us it would be delivered the next day and I decided that there was no point worrying. What will be, will be.

From Sharm El-Sheikh it was a three-hour coach ride up to the hotel near Mount Sinai, which was where we were to spend our first night. Some people had got their luggage (not me, unfortunately) so there was a lot of chatter about who could lend what to whom. Everyone's main concern was that we would be freezing the next morning as we set off to climb up that amazing mountain. Once we arrived at our hotel there was a lot of swapping and a little bit of moaning but after a quick supper we all settled down for an early night. I think everyone was excited and terrified in equal measure of what lay ahead.

Mount Sinai is one of the most important sites for Jews, Christians and Muslims alike. It was where, during the Jewish exile from slavery in Egypt (commemorated every year at Passover), Moses received the Torah which included, most famously, the Ten Commandments.

We were awoken at 3.30 a.m. to discover that the remaining luggage had arrived. There was a quick reshuffle as everyone returned what had been borrowed the night before, grabbed a breakfast bag and climbed back onto the coaches for the short journey to the base of the mountain itself.

It was still dark when we arrived and, togged up with all my thermals, I set off with the group of walkers I had been assigned to trek with. (There were three different groups to allow for different abilities.) At the base of the mountain is the monastery of St Katherine's or, more correctly, the Sacred Monastery of the God-Trodden Mount Sinai. It was built in the early sixth century and is still a working monastery, the oldest one in the world I believe. Everyone who visits Mount Sinai has to pay a fee to support the monastery and the nature reserve around it, the whole area being a UNESCO world heritage site.

Our group had already been registered and the necessary fees paid so we did not have to wait around for long and within a very short time we set out walking. You can either take the Camel Path from the north-east corner of the monastery, or the Steps of Repentance from the south-east corner. It had been decided that we would go up the path rather than clamber up

3,750 stone steps that go up to the top in a horribly steep, almost-straight line.

As the name suggests, there were assorted ropey-looking camels on the Camel Path with their eager handlers offering 'air-conditioned taxi rides' to the top. (Actually, the camels can't go all the way to the top because even if you don't take the Steps of Repentance from the bottom, you still have to climb a few steep flights of steps to make the summit.) I had only ever seen a camel in a zoo before but these ones did not look as well fed. I was not remotely tempted to do anything other than get up the mountain under my own steam.

The path is quite wide and wends up with long switch-backs. It is easy to follow but it is a good two and a half to three hours' climb and it was far from being freezing. I was boiling. How I got to the top I will never know, but I did – and immediately burst into tears. It was amazing.

The sun was just coming up and you could see out for miles and miles across the desert with hardly any sign of civilization – just strange rock formations and lots and lots of sand. Mount Sinai is 2,285 metres high and is surrounded by even higher peaks, including Mount Katherine, the highest peak in Egypt. But the fact that Sinai is the baby of the range did not take away from my overwhelming sense of achievement.

Once all of us had made it onto the summit, the rabbi who was with us, Barry Marcus, said a few prayers and blew the 'shofar' that he carried with him. It was completely magical. There is a small mosque at the summit as well as a tiny Greek Orthodox chapel but we didn't visit them (I think the chapel was closed anyway). For me, it was enough to stand and marvel.

I found the descent a little easier but it still took several hours before we were all back on the coaches and heading off into the desert for lunch and the start of the trek proper. I was already exhausted but exhilarated. I felt much better after lunch and was eager to get going.

Each group was accompanied by an Israeli army-trained guide and a medic and the guide set the pace that he thought worked best for us all. I was in the slowest group but that suited me well as I had time to take in the extraordinary scenery we travelled through, and I am convinced that being so small meant I had to take two strides to equal everyone else's one!

I had been nervous about sleeping in a communal tent but, that night, never having done anything so physical before, I was asleep before I was even aware of climbing into my sleeping bag and settling down.

For the next few days the routine was the same, even if the terrain was dramatically different. We would get up early and set out at 7.00 a.m. Lunch would be around midday – delivered by camel – and we would arrive at our new campsite (already set up with supper cooking) at around 5.00 p.m. The evenings close in early so we had to be set up before darkness fell and the most dazzling canopy of stars you can imagine filled the sky.

We averaged about nineteen kilometres a day (some days were shorter than others) but there was a lot of climbing and it was very, very hot. The temperatures in the Sinai in November are around the eighties during the day and, because it hadn't rained for ten years, the air was unbelievably dry. It was not comfortable, and it certainly was not easy, but the camaraderie was huge and I met some amazing people of all different ages.

Our last day of trekking was on the Friday and the aim was to reach Eilat and the luxury of the Princess Hotel in time for a special Shabbat celebration meal. We set off from the rugged Wadi Malacha and a few strenuous hours later we arrived on the shore of the Red Sea where a delicious brunch was waiting for us. The hard work was over and never has the prospect of a shower been so thrilling. There was a lot of backslapping, kissing and hugging and very few dry eyes. We were all elated, not least because we had raised, between us, something like £300,000 for One to One.

Everyone was very excited as we climbed aboard the coaches for the journey up to the Israeli border and on to Eilat (about sixty-five kilometres along the coast road). I knew that Harold had flown in and was waiting for me, but I didn't know that he had arranged a surprise cocktail party for all the trekkers. It was a typically thoughtful gesture from my generous husband.

I was very sad that Harold could not join in the actual trekking but the saddest thing of all was that he never had the opportunity to stand on top of Mount Sinai and view the world he had read about since he was a small boy. (Harold has always been more frum than me and he would have loved the whole thing.) I don't have the words to describe what it is like and photos do not do it justice. It was the most amazing experience of my life.

I did a further four treks over the succeeding years and each and every one was special. On the second trek I wore my boots from the first and I think they must have stretched (or I must have shrunk) as they felt a little big. By the end of the first day both of my feet were one big blister. Our group medic, who was an anaesthetist, just put Compeed blister plasters on my feet and told me to lie down!

The next day we were walking along a very high, narrow ridge and my feet were so terrible that I lost my balance. It was only thanks to one well-placed rock that I did not end up tumbling down the mountain. I did cut my head open, mind you, and there was blood everywhere. Our medic decided I needed my head stitched but said he couldn't do it because he had never done anything like that. He bandaged me up in the short term and when we got to camp they put out an SOS and a jeep appeared from somewhere.

We were in the middle of the desert but 'civilization' (even if not as we know it) is never too far away. On this occasion they took me to a nearby 'moshav', which is a bit like a small kibbutz. I was greeted by a lovely nurse who said she could easily sew me up but it would involve cutting away some of my hair. I went ballistic: I have such thick hair it would take two seconds to cover any gap, but my hair is my one vanity. The nurse smiled and ignored me completely. She cut my hair, stitched me up and sent me back to the camp with a big headache and an ever bigger dose of painkillers.

The next day I carried on with the trek but I had a problem breathing and it was decided that I should go to the hospital in Eilat. Another SOS, another jeep. When you are trekking you lose all sense of time, but at the hospital they wanted to check my cognitive awareness and the first question they asked was, 'What day of the week is it?' I didn't have a clue, no idea at all. They then became concerned that I was concussed. Luckily for me, various checks proved I was not, and I was allowed to go back to the camp. When I told my story about not knowing what day of the week it was, everyone thought it hilarious because they had no idea either!

Another year we had a meeting in London about that year's trek, and were told that there was one particular spot where you could either abseil down a cliff or take a four-hour detour. I decided that I would abseil. I have to tell you that at that point I was terrified of heights but I knew only too well what four hours of extra trekking would involve.

Rita Eker, the trek organiser, arranged for us to have a training session at the Chepstow Quarry. She booked a bus to take us to Wales and I could not stop quaking for the entire journey. When we got there I thought it would be better to get it over and done with, rather than standing on the edge of the cliff fretting. I asked to go first. That is my way of dealing with anything that I am anxious about. 'Just do it,' I always tell myself.

I abseiled down the cliff face and was as exhilarated as if I had climbed up Mount Everest. I begged to do it again. Harold did it too, of course, and afterwards we felt so good that we did it again on a London tower with David and Jill. It meant that when, on the actual trek, we got to the rock wall in the desert I was not concerned at all. There was an amazing man on that trek who was ninety years old, so he and I did it together. It was wonderful and I am now absolutely fine with heights.

We did not always follow the same route or schedule and the next time I climbed Mount Sinai it was during the day and via the gruelling Steps of Repentance. I have never, ever been so shattered as when I reached the top, but I did get to see the view at sunset rather than sunrise. What made that expedition especially memorable, though, was that the day we climbed Mount Sinai was the 'yahrzeit' of my mother's death and the rabbi said prayers for her as we looked out towards the Promised Land. As we descended the mountain by torchlight (another magical experience) I could not stop crying.

Harold always came to meet me at the end of the treks, and the one that was based more in Jordan and east Israel, including the ancient fortress settlement of Masada, was no exception. Masada is an amazing ruin, but what makes it famous is the mass suicide of the 960 rebels who resisted a Roman siege there in the first century AD.

There has been a lot written about Masada as the siege was recorded by a Jewish historian of the day, Joseph ben Matityahu, who was renamed by the Romans, Titus Flavius

Josephus. His report said that, because suicide is against Jewish law, the Masada rebels drew lots and killed each other in turn so that only the last man would be obliged to take his own life. (Murder is against the Torah too, but I suppose it must be the lesser of two evils.) I think there is some debate about all that now, but Masada is still a revered place and has become one of the most popular tourist destinations in Israel.

I find Masada very impressive and unbelievably moving and, what is more, you get the most fantastic views over the Judaean Desert and out to the Dead Sea. That year we did not take the usual Snake Path (so called because it is very narrow and windy), but climbed the steep siege ramp that the Romans built to scale the mountain all those years ago. And who was at the top to meet me? Thanks to modern engineering, Harold had made the excursion courtesy of the cable car. I did not care how he had got there; I was just so excited to see him.

Over the years I managed to raise a lot of money for the One to One Project, mainly because all our business associates were so very generous. I think they knew what a huge undertaking every trek was for me physically and were wonderful in the support they offered. And while I know the money went to a good cause, the greatest payback for me was the amazing sense of achievement I had from taking part in the project. The treks I did were totally life-enhancing and unforgettable.

CHAPTER TEN

The year after my first trek Jill announced that she was engaged. Our darling daughter had managed to fall in love with 'the only non-Jew in New York' and Harold was not best pleased. He said he was not going to the wedding; I said he was. We went and it was a gorgeous affair.

Jill's Michael – Michael Traina – has been in fabrics all his life and is a very nice man. They had the most wonderful wedding in the garden of his aunt's stunning New Jersey home. Jill made a beautiful bride and it was a very happy day.

We were thrilled when we learned that the new Mr and Mrs Traina were planning to come to live in England and in September of that year they arrived. Jill took over as manager of the Knightsbridge shop and Michael set up a fabric business in Bushey, which he runs to this day. (Sadly, the marriage did not last and they split up when their daughter, Rachel, was still very young.)

Business for us continued to do well and both Rigby & Peller shops were so busy that we decided to open another, this time in Barnet, north London. The Brent Cross Shopping Centre had recently been renovated and expanded and had attracted a suitable number of up-market names that we felt sat well with Rigby & Peller. It was a big step for us because the rent and service charges were high (someone had to pay for the parking) and the business rates were a further £120,000 a year. We leased just one unit, but it in the end it proved to be too small and it was not viable to take on another. There was a break clause in the lease after five years and we took it.

Meanwhile we had been approached by the British Airports Authority (BAA) who wanted us to put a Rigby & Peller store into Heathrow's Terminal Three, which had been renovated a few years previously at a cost of over £110 million. We had many discussions about having a presence at Heathrow and decided it was worth a try. There was no fixed rent as such because with BAA you paid a percentage of your turnover. That meant we had all the upfront costs of submitting the tender document (which was huge and drove poor David mad), as well as the costs of building and fitting out the store. We did it because we thought it would be good and we tried our very best to make it work.

There were all sorts of obstacles for a business like ours. The terminal shops had to be open from six in the morning until midnight which meant we had to have more staff than usual; and all the staff had to have references that went back five years because they were working 'airside' (beyond security). On top of that our staff needed to be trained fitters because our fitting service is a huge part of what sets Rigby & Peller apart.

Then there was the question of delivery. We could not deliver directly to the shop: everything had to go to a central warehouse which added another strand to the administration and a headache factor when things went astray. There was also a marketing issue. Our shop was tucked away but there were very strict controls on what you could and could not do to promote your business within the terminal.

Funnily enough, the one thing we were concerned about was not an issue. You would not believe how many women walked into the shop and said, 'I've forgotten to pack a bra', or 'I need a swimsuit because I've left mine at home'. We also had quite a few clued-up customers. A lot of women who shopped in Rigby & Peller in Knightsbridge were regular travellers (they don't call it the 'Tiara Triangle' for nothing) and very savvy. They knew of the price differential (airside purchases are VAT-free for non-EU destinations). So they would order in town and pick up and pay for the goods on their way through the airport. We used to have to send all sorts of things out to Heathrow!

We gave it our best shot for about three years but then, in mutual agreement with BAA, we pulled out and looked for other avenues where we could expand.

Most of us know that, 'if you want something done, ask a busy person', so I can only assume that the Royal Marsden Early Diagnostic Unit decided to apply that principle when they approached me to see if I could help – as I had once before.

In 1982 I had set up a campaign to save the unit when I learned that it was threatened with closure. The Royal Marsden was facing a deficit of £750,000 at the time and the hospital governors thought to save money by closing the unit – in spite of the fact that it screened 10,000 women a year.

Through one of my customers, Frances Green, who was in charge of the renovations at Lambeth Palace, I had met the Archbishop of Canterbury's wife, Rosalind Runcie. We had had dinner together on several occasions and I decided to ask Rosalind to help. It was not just because I was already really busy with the Soviet Jewry Campaign, but also because I knew that Rosalind would generate press interest. She was delighted to get involved.

We decided to start off simply by setting up a petition asking the hospital governors to reconsider their decision. Rosalind launched the petition on Tuesday 23 November at what was then the Contour shop in Knightsbridge. On the same day, Baroness Lena Jeger stood up in the House of Lords, 'To ask Her Majesty's Government whether they will make a statement on the Early Diagnostic Unit at the Royal Marsden Hospital...'

Rosalind and I knew that between us, we could call on other impressive names for support. Rosamond Cullen, wife of Lord Cullen, who was one of the Appeal Lords in the House of Lords, was a faithful Contour customer, as was Dame Adelaide Doughty who was on the Grand Council of the Cancer Research Campaign. Lady Mary Soames (Winston Churchill's youngest child) and Elizabeth Roskill, married to the brilliant Lord Roskill, a peer and lawyer on the Judicial Committee of the Privy Council, also signed.

As an aside, Lady Roskill was great fun and often used to bring me sourdough bread. I never had the heart to tell her sourdough was not my favourite as she thought it the most delicious bread ever! I still have numerous postcards she sent me from all over the world, telling me what she was up to and reporting on the state of her husband's health. They are very entertaining, although not easy to read, as Elizabeth liked to cram as much information as possible into the smallest space in her elegant, flowery handwriting. Lord Roskill was an extremely important man and I often wondered what he would have thought had he known quite how much I knew about his indigestion!

We had four hundred signatures at the end of our first day in Knightsbridge alone and the following day put copies of the petition at our Contour shop in the Whitgift Centre in Croydon and at Rigby & Peller in South Molton Street.

We had planned to run the petition for three weeks but within just seven days our petition had served its purpose. On

Tuesday 30 November the Secretary of State for Social Services announced a reprieve for the unit. Norman Fowler said he had decided that it should not close immediately and that the government would provide £155,000 a year to fund the unit for the next four years. He told the House of Commons that the matter would be reviewed in 1986 when the first results of an investigation into the value of screening for breast cancer had become available.

We had won – and all within the space of a week!

I decided it would be only right to make an appointment so we could thank Mr Fowler for his decision. You can imagine how surprised I was when his office said, 'No. We don't do things like that.' I thought that was really stupid: the department was always being blamed for something or other and we just wanted to say a huge thank you and celebrate one of their better decisions.

By now my old friend Bernard Weatherill was Speaker of the House of Commons, so I rang to see if he could help. Bernard agreed that thanks were in order. 'Don't worry, June. Now that I am Speaker, if I invite Norman to come to my office, he is obliged to do so. Leave it to me.' As always, Bernard was as good as his word. He arranged to host a small reception for us in his office and Norman Fowler put in an appearance to receive our thanks. It was, all in all, very satisfying.

I maintained my links with the Royal Marsden Early Diagnostic Unit over the years and in 1997 was very taken when a young nurse, Nikki Burch, came up with what I thought was a brilliant idea. Nikki was concerned that too many women – especially young women – were not 'breast aware' (she had noticed that lots of people completely ignored the leaflets that were available). Nikki's solution – so simple but so clever – was to put advisory tags on bras.

Marks & Spencer, I believe, had turned down the chance to sponsor the project but we leapt at it. It was the year that Harold and I were celebrating being in business together for thirty-five years and we thought it was a very positive campaign to throw our weight behind. We had a million labels printed with 'Be Breast Aware' on one side and instructions on what to look for on the other. For the next few months, every Rigby & Peller bra and every Fantasie bra sold in the country carried one of our swing tags. Between the two brands we covered more than 1,500 outlets nationwide, so the scope was huge.

We had fantastic support for the campaign, including a lovely letter from Linda McCartney who could not attend the launch but sent the following message:

> Breast Cancer can strike any woman at any time. It does not respect the young and healthy, who can be easily duped into believing that they are immune from this dreadful disease. Like older women, they must regularly examine themselves and be alert to any changes in their breasts. This won't prevent them from getting the disease, but it will hugely increase their chances of successfully fighting it.

Mrs McCartney's message is especially poignant because the following year she died, having battled breast cancer for years.

We decided to hold a launch party at our Conduit Street shop and wanted to use a young model to stress the point we were trying to make. Tessa Dahl (Roald Dahl's daughter) was a friend of mine, having been a Contour and then Rigby & Peller customer for many years. Her beautiful daughter, Sophie, was only young at the time of the campaign but already boasted a curvaceous figure and a 38DD bust. She was just the sort of girl we needed. When I asked her if she would model a range of bras, complete with our Breast Awareness tag, she jumped at the chance. It must have been one of Sophie's first-ever modelling jobs (if not the first) but she refused to take any payment. She was really amazing.

We got a lot of press coverage and most of the papers quoted Sophie: 'I am nineteen and I've never checked my breasts before. I'm not sure I would even know what to do.' It was perfect publicity and emphasised how necessary the campaign was. It is so important to check your breasts; you must be in control of your own destiny.

We were very proud of our involvement in the campaign and if it helped to save even one woman, the million labels we put out there were worth it.

Not long after the Breast Awareness launch Sophie was 'discovered' by Isabella Blow and went on to have a fabulous career working for *Vogue* and the top designers and photographers. She is now a wife, mother and writer and is a gorgeous girl in every which way.

It must have been around the same time as the Breast Awareness campaign that Harold and I decided we should move. We absolutely loved our home in Croydon but we knew that we were not south Londoners at heart. St John's Wood was the obvious choice, because we had moved from the Catford Synagogue to become members of the St John's Wood Synagogue several years before. My parents had been members for years and the lights in the new synagogue are dedicated to my father.

Belonging to a synagogue is very important to us for lots of reasons, not least because the fees that you pay give you burial rights. Cremation is not allowed under Jewish law, and when we die we are buried in a plain wooden box – a box without any ornamentation whatsoever. It doesn't matter if you are hugely wealthy or very poor: we all go to our maker in a meagre coffin. And it is quick. (You are buried, usually, within twenty-four hours of death.) A Jewish funeral is simple but very, very moving. The coffin goes on a trolley with a velvet cloth over the top and after the service the body is wheeled out to the grave. Once the coffin has been lowered the men spade the earth on top: it is considered an honour to participate in the burial by taking a turn to shovel soil onto the coffin. And then we say what is perhaps the most famous Jewish prayer of all, the 'kaddish'. It is an ancient memorial prayer that has been uttered by Jewish mourners around the world for centuries and it always makes me cry.

We started looking at flats in St John's Wood but suddenly realised that if we moved to a flat there would not be enough room to put in a gym. And where do you park in St John's Wood? The other concern was that we wanted to be close to the children. David and Simona were living in Stanmore; Jill and Michael were near Watford.

I kept up my routine of going to the Bimal gym twice a week and afterwards would often go up to Stanmore to see Simona and our first beautiful granddaughter, Hannah. (We now have three beautiful granddaughters – Hannah, her sister Emily, and Jill's Rachel. How lucky are we?)

One day I was in Stanmore and passed an estate agent where there was an advertisement in the window that caught my eye. It was for a lovely big bungalow in a secluded close in Bushey Heath. I went in and asked to see it that afternoon. Harold was working so Simona kindly came with me and Hannah, who was only a few months old at the time, came too. The decoration was hateful but it was the most spacious bungalow I had ever seen and had the potential to be beautiful. I think Simona was rather surprised when I said, 'I could live here.'

When David and Harold came in from work they could not believe I had made up my mind so quickly. And when Harold came to see the house he was not taken with the location at all. He liked the close well enough but not the road that led to it. To cut a long story short (well, not that long), we bought the house and have not looked back since. It is perfect being close to the children and I love the fact that we live in the heart of a Jewish community.

The one downside about moving away from Croydon was that I had to lose my wonderful cleaner, Pat Prignits. Pat came to us after Hattie left and had been with us for years, but our new home was too far away from hers to travel to on a daily basis. She did come to live with us for a few days when we moved to help us get everything sorted and I thought she would die of unhappiness when we had to say goodbye.

Pat was not the fastest worker, but she was immaculate – and I do require immaculate. She was really the most extra- ordinarily kind and selfless woman. She used to work for me for six hours a day and then go straight away to cook a meal for her mother-in-law. She was wonderful and I thought it particularly unfair that when her mother-in-law died she left nothing at all to Pat. Everything went to Pat's brother-in-law in Canada who never did anything for his mother. Aren't people strange?

We quickly settled into our new home so we could go back to concentrating on the business. Our overseas sales of Rigby & Peller continued to do well and we had an approach from a Japanese company who thought they might like to have Rigby & Peller underwear too. A couple of very correct gentlemen came to see us and we began the lengthy process of the interview. They did not speak English and we do not speak

Japanese so everything had to be done through an interpreter. I thought I would lose the will to live. It was agony. We finally got through all the business matters and then we invited the two gentlemen to have lunch with us in Harrods. The minute our guests were presented with the menu they understood enough English to be able to order the most expensive items! Dover Sole, they knew about that, and they knew which wine would go perfectly with it. They could not speak English but somehow they had learned how to read it well enough to order a fine meal. It amused us greatly but in the end we did not go any further in establishing a Japanese outlet. (Currently our only Asian outlets are in China and Hong Kong.)

The bespoke side of the business has continued to do well and, over the years, we have had some unusual requests. One came from a gentleman whose wife was a keen Newcastle United fan. As a surprise for her birthday he ordered a custom-made corset in the team's black and white stripe, with a big blue star on the front. He did not know his wife's size so we had to estimate it from his description, which we must have done well because it did not came back to be altered! When he saw the corset, the husband decided that his wife should have matching knickers as well, so the workroom set to and produced a beautiful pair of French knickers, also in the Newcastle United colours.

The girls in the workroom are always wonderful with such requests and never bat an eyelid if someone asks for something unusual. And the workroom in Knightsbridge is still the domain of one of the young seamstresses we inherited with Rigby & Peller, Laura Day, and another, Nicky Bush, who joined us soon after.

I was very touched recently when someone asked Nicky what it was like working for Rigby & Peller (which she has done for thirty-two years). 'We're a family,' was her reply. And it is true. We have always believed that the people who work for you are your gold-dust and our 'family' has included some amazing people over the years. It would be impossible to tell you about all of them, but one or two have been very special indeed.

Our doorman, Ted Chinner, comes to mind immediately, followed closely by Clyne Cullen, who worked with us in the early days in Croydon and became the manager of Contour in Knightsbridge. Clyne was a marvellous fitter and a very good manager and when she left to do other things I was very upset.

Another member of staff whom we inherited with Rigby & Peller was Madeleine Spry, known to everyone, including us, as Mrs Spry. (I cannot imagine anyone ever calling her Maddy.) Mrs Spry looked after our made-to-measure customers, who sometimes need two or even three fittings, and she was perfect for the job. She was an absolute lady through and through and as many of our customers are too, Mrs Spry knew exactly how to treat them.

And then there was Kathy Williams, who came to us originally as a cleaner. Kathy lived in the country, so it was a huge 'schlep' into Knightsbridge. She had to walk across fields in her wellies to catch the early bus every morning to get to the shop in time to clean it before we opened. After a few years Kathy asked if she could train to be a bra-fitter and, of course, we said yes. She became a Rigby & Peller assistant and ended up as the Knightsbridge shop manager. The customers adored her, especially the Arab customers, some of whom would only come into the shop if they knew Kathy would be there. The instructions were quite clear: if Kathy was at lunch and any Arabs came in she was to be told immediately, wherever she was. Kathy was a big, big woman but she would fly up the stairs like lightning and 'Madam' would be sorted. According to Kathy, there wasn't anything that Rigby & Peller could not do, and the fact that sometimes we had difficulty coming up with what she had promised is another story. As far as Kathy was concerned, whatever the customer wanted, the customer had. She used to live and breathe Rigby & Peller – we were her life – and she was absolutely fantastic.

Kathy's sales tactics were sometimes interesting, mind you. There was an occasion when she was selling a basque to an up-market and seemingly intelligent client and Kathy thought a little more persuasion was required. 'Do you know,' Kathy said to the woman in a conspiratorial sort of way, 'we had Scarlett O'Hara in last week and she bought two.' Kathy obviously wasn't thinking, or maybe did not realise that Scarlett O'Hara is a fictitious character and Vivien Leigh, who played the part in *Gone With The Wind*, was a long time dead. No matter, the customer was obviously impressed as she bought two basques and, I believe, ordered a third!

Kathy was hugely special but eventually she had trouble with her legs and had to retire. We missed her so much and even up to a few years ago the Saudi King's family continued to ask for her.

Inevitably, as we developed more Rigby & Peller stores (next up was one in the Bluewater Shopping Centre in Stone in Kent), there was less interaction with the staff, but we have always done what we can to retain good relationships. We hold Christmas parties and that sort of thing, one of the most memorable being when we took everyone for dinner and a night of greyhound races at Wembley. We even sponsored one of the races and it tickles me still when I see the photo that was taken when I had to present the prize to the winner of the Rigby & Peller Stakes.

We have always trained our staff well. When we first opened Contour in Knightsbridge Harold decided to add a new strand to the training that, I confess, would never have occurred to me. He was worried that a few members of staff – brilliant fitters though they were – did not speak well enough to put them at ease with some of our more up-market clients. My enterprising husband's answer was to arrange a course of elocution lessons for everybody!

Harold found a wonderful woman to come into the shop one evening a week for several weeks to teach the girls how to speak the Queen's English. Far from being upset, everyone thought it was a great opportunity and attended the classes with good heart. The exercises, which were in the 'how now brown cow' mould, generated a lot of fun but, more importantly, the lessons achieved what Harold hoped they would. They really did give the women a new level of confidence.

When it came to the more conventional form of training for lingerie staff, I used to do some but not all, and we have always had someone in charge of fitting to go round all the shops.

I think the key thing when you are looking for someone to work in lingerie is a good personality. You have to have someone who gets on well with people because they are fitting customers with the most intimate items of clothing. And then, some people are just natural salespeople. We have a member of staff like that in Knightsbridge at the moment. Ulla left Rigby & Peller for family reasons but, luckily for us, came back as soon as she could. In her first morning back at work Ulla sold someone £700 worth of goods. That's natural salesmanship!

In 1999 we launched our first website. It was the hardest thing to get right and is the subject of many discussions even now. We knew we had to have online presence but our strengths are fitting and customer service. You can translate the second into e-commerce but how do you translate the first? Our first website was really a guide to where you could find our shops and examples of what we sold, but as internet shopping became more popular we had to adapt. We added more elaborate 'help pages' and advice alongside a selective product range. Initially we thought of offering products so that existing customers could reorder what they had already bought in store but, of course, we picked up new business too. The internet has really tested us and the hardest job, even now, is to try to get the online experience to mirror the in-store experience. We keep trying!

Expansion also meant we had to come up with all sorts of things we had never had to think about before, such as a professional and extensive staff manual. Harold was always full of good ideas, as are the children, and we put together a wonderful book telling new staff what we wanted from them; what they could expect from us; plus all the important but boring things such as health and safety and fire extinguishers, etc etc.

Harold also came up with a couple of acronyms which still amuse me, but they are all about good customer service, which is so important. E-A-G-E-R stands for Eye Contact, Approach, Greet, Entice and Reform, the theory being that if you have served your customer well they will be 'reformed' and will return to shop at Rigby & Peller – but in our case it also works literally because by the time they leave us every customer should have a gorgeous new shape. S-M-I-L-E is also aimed at customer satisfaction and stands for Satisfy, Motivate, Identify, Laud, Encourage. A good motto for life, don't you think?

CHAPTER ELEVEN

One of the most important lessons I learned through my involvement with the Women's Campaign for Soviet Jewry is that you mustn't wait for someone to come to you; you have to do the approaching – and that applies to all branches of the media. I learned to be fearless in promoting Rigby & Peller and often appeared on LBC, the London-based national talk and phone-in radio station. LBC was the UK's first licensed commercial radio station (they opened a week before Capital Radio) and they were always open to good ideas and hungry for contributors, so I rang them often.

I did lots of radio and press interviews but one of my first television experiences was on the popular game show, *What's My Line?*. The programme was based on an American series of the same name and the idea was that different guests did a short mime to suggest what their job was (I mimed lacing a corset which raised a lot of laughter). The panellists then had the chance to ask questions to help them solve the puzzle. By the time I got involved, Eammon Andrews was the host and they had different regular panellists including Ernie Wise, Angela Rippon and Jeffrey Archer. It was a lot of fun and even more so for me when I stumped them! I still have a certificate somewhere congratulating me for defeating the panel.

I also have happy memories of appearing on the Michael Barrymore show. Michael's wife, Cheryl, was a very good customer and he always came in with her when she was buying lingerie. Michael would sit outside the fitting room sipping coffee and he always made sure there was a lot of banter and silliness. Then one day, to my surprise and delight, he asked me to appear on his programme. Michael was hosting a very popular chat show at the time and he interviewed me about lingerie in general and Rigby & Peller in particular. He was still married to Cheryl at that stage, but a little while later their life went horribly and very publicly wrong. I was very sad about what happened subsequently. Cheryl died when she was only fifty-five and Michael – well, his story does not need retelling here. All I will say is that when we knew them, we thought Michael and Cheryl were the closest, most wonderful couple ever.

I cannot remember any details of the interview I did for the Channel Four breakfast programme except that I was interviewed by a pair of socks! The socks were puppets and the whole thing was done on a bed. What I do remember is that I turned down the chance to ride motorbike pillion. When the station rang to ask if I would appear on the show they said they would send a motorbike to pick me up. I have already admitted that I am very fussy and that I have a thing about my hair, so you can imagine how unimpressed I was at the thought of having to stick on a crash helmet and weave through the grime of London. They sent a car. It was only later when I told the story to David that I had second thoughts. 'Mum,' he said, 'you've really missed out. You'd have loved it.' He was so convinced that he convinced *me*. (Mind you, had I really wanted to, I could easily have arranged such a trip for myself but somehow I never got around to it!)

I also went up often to do *This Morning* in the days when it was produced in Liverpool (now ITV do it from London). If ever there was a bra story (and you wouldn't believe how often there was a bra story), there I would be. They would fly me up to Manchester and a car would pick me up and take me to the studios in Liverpool. The most memorable journey was the day I had to share the car with an Elvis look-alike. When he discovered we were on the same plane back to London he asked if he could sit next to me. It turned out he had never flown before and was very, very nervous. How could I say no?

We both finished our slots on the programme and the car took us back to the airport. My Elvis was a real gentleman and insisted on carrying my sample case. Normally, I would be very grateful for such a courtesy but in this instance I was not so sure because he was wearing a garish, over-the-top Elvis outfit, complete with huge sunglasses. I had no option but to totter alongside, which I found hugely embarrassing as, of course, everyone was staring at him. In desperation I thought I might shake him off if I said I needed the Ladies. That was a foolish assumption! Elvis simply stood outside and waited for me. In the end, I bought him a sandwich and a coffee and slipped away until it was time to go to the gate.

On another occasion I had a phone call from the *This Morning* wardrobe department asking if I could take some underwear up for Judy Finnegan to try. The problem was that no one knew what size Judy was because she would never divulge any personal information. (I was told that the wardrobe crew used to buy clothes that they thought would fit but they always cut out the size labels so as not to upset her.)

It was suggested that I should watch a few programmes, study Judy closely and make an estimate that way. And that is what I did. I took various samples with me the next time

I went but it took some convincing to get Judy to allow me into her dressing room. Eventually she did let me in but it was certainly not one of my best fitting experiences. It was all absurdly quick! I still find it strange that someone who is so versed in being in front of a camera should have so little self-confidence in her own body.

My most memorable television experience was working with the gorgeous fashion stylist Gok Wan, on the first series of *How to Look Good Naked* – or as the crew called it HTLGN. I did eight programmes with Gok and it was truly wonderful. He was so sympathetic to the women who featured in the programmes and really showed them not only how to make the most of themselves, but – more importantly – how to like themselves. Luckily for Rigby & Peller, Gok really understands the importance of underwear and is dead against liposuction and any form of cosmetic surgery. He is one of the few men I have ever met who knows that the right underwear can make an outfit look great.

I was really touched when I read an interview Gok did during the series in which he said that he had always taken his clients to Rigby & Peller. If that was not enough, he added, 'If you get the opportunity to meet the Queen of Undies, owner of Rigby & Peller, June Kenton, then that in itself is a day out.' How lovely is that?

We didn't film in the shop because there was not enough room and any filming is very time consuming, so the production company built a mock fitting room in a studio near Islington. Anyone who knows anything about television will know that there is a lot (and I mean a *lot*) of material filmed that is never used, which means that somewhere there must be hours of wonderful moments of HTLGN that never made it to the screen. It was such fun.

On screen Gok would always refer to me as 'The Grande Dame of Underwear' or the 'Queen of Undies', but to my face he called me 'my second mum' – a great honour because he adores his real mum. (Gok's mother is English, his Dad is from Hong Kong and Gok was born and brought up in Leicestershire.) I think what makes Gok so totally sympathetic is that when he was young, besides being of mixed race, he was sensitive, tall, gay and fat: a bully-magnet, if ever there was one – as the poor boy learned to his cost. But Gok's own trials meant that when he was making HTLGN he really understood what the women felt like when they stood in front of a mirror and hated what they saw. It seems amazing now because he's so lean and fit, but I read a brilliant article about Gok in the *Guardian* (just before his next big show *Miss Naked Beauty* came out), and in that he said that being fat had an effect on '…everything: my personality, how people reacted to me, what I wore, everything. When you sit down with someone who's twenty-one stone you have certain expectations of what they're like: stupid, lazy or really funny.' Gok is very funny but is a long way from being stupid or lazy; in fact, he is really switched on and can be quite hyper if anything!

I loved working with Gok and of course it was wonderful for Rigby & Peller. His agent is a lovely woman called Carol Hayes, and through her he became very interested in our Jewish traditions. I knew how fascinated he was because he was always asking questions, but it did not stop me being surprised when Gok said that he wanted to come to us for Friday dinner and that he wanted to light the Shabbat candles. I explained that it is usually the women who light the candles, but then I thought, 'Well…' The family was thrilled when Gok came to us (especially my young granddaughters). We found a napkin to cover his head, I found some spare candles for him to light and so Gok got to play out his own version of our Friday night ritual. It was lovely and very touching because he was so interested in the whole tradition.

Gok went on to make another four series of HTLGN, but the format changed so I was let off the hook. I watched every programme though – of course I did – not only because I love Gok but because I really agree with what he preaches: every woman can look and feel amazing without going under the knife. Like him, I am against cosmetic surgery and know, from years of experience, why breast enhancement is a bad idea. Silicone implants are often solid and do not sit naturally in a bra, and there are so many health risks if things go wrong. Besides which, these days there are amazing bras that can turn an insignificant bust into something that really stands out and makes a statement!

Breast reduction, on the other hand, is a completely different story. I do not think of breast reduction as cosmetic surgery. Over-large breasts can cause back and shoulder problems and various other health issues, so when my own Jill decided that she was going to have the operation I was relieved. Jill had big boobs from a very early age and suffered all sorts of complications because of them over the years, even though she has always worn good, properly fitted bras (obviously!). We used to talk about Jill having a reduction, but it is a very personal decision: when she finally made it, there was no stopping her. The operation has been a fantastic success – Jill went down to a D-cup from an FF-cup and immediately said goodbye to her problems.

The way Jill dealt with the operation once she had decided to go ahead is typical of the way she works. Jill is very much a 'now' person and is wonderful at getting things done. She took over from me as head of Public Relations at Rigby &

Peller in the early 2000s and did it extremely well. I always tell her that she had a good teacher, but the truth is she is a natural.

She developed a very good relationship with the press and with the publicity department of 20th Century Fox and other film production companies. It was down to Jill that, when *Moulin Rouge* premiered in London, we had live mannequins in the Knightsbridge shop window dressed as if they had just stepped off the Boulevard de Clichy.

Jill was also responsible for Rigby & Peller's cameo appearance in the second Bridget Jones film, *The Edge of Reason*. The production company that was making the film approached us, via Jill, and asked if they could use Rigby & Peller for the scene where Bridget Jones has to find the right underwear to help her squeeze into a ball dress (a completely horrific yellow satin affair). Jill, never short of chutzpah, said she would be happy to offer the Conduit Street shop but that she wanted a certain amount of product placement and wanted to be in the scene herself! Harold and David did the negotiation and struck a deal which stated that the production company would pay a location cost for the filming and, if the Rigby & Peller name was shown for less than a specified length of time, there would be a financial penalty. The company met the agreement in full. We got £10,000 for the disruption of business for the day, the Rigby & Peller name appeared on a fake window and, if you look closely enough, Jill is in the background talking to a 'customer'. Success all round.

It was around the same time that I was invited to a reception for businesswomen at Buckingham Palace. I had just had an operation on my foot – the joints between my toes and my foot were loose and had to be screwed into place – so I couldn't walk. I really wanted to go and Nicky Thomas, our trainer's wife and our masseuse, kindly agreed to come and push me in a wheelchair. I managed to get out of the chair for long enough to hobble down the line to curtsey and shake hands with the Royal Family, but at the end of it I got back into the wheelchair as quickly as I could. There were hundreds of people at the event so I was very surprised when the Princess Royal came to find me to check that I was all right. She was not a Rigby & Peller bespoke customer and I had not served her personally, so I was very touched that she made such a special effort.

The children were now on the board of Rigby & Peller with Harold and me, David having joined in 1993 and Jill in 2001, and we all wanted to move the business forward. The big problem was that we weren't sure how to go about it. After a lot of chat around the kitchen table – we were a family business after all – we decided that we needed outside help. On one of my treks I had made friends with a lovely woman from 'up north' called Hilary Miller. When you are trekking there is a lot of time to chat and Hilary liked to chat about her husband, whom she always referred to as 'my Morris'. (Hilary talked about 'my Morris' a lot.) I learned that he was an accountant by profession but had his fingers in an assortment of pies and was in great demand.

Hilary and I kept in touch and once, after she had told me yet another long and involved story about 'my Morris', I said, 'You know something Hilary, maybe we should meet your Morris. We're looking for a new pair of eyes to help us and he might be the man for us.' And he was. Harold and I went up to Leeds to meet Morris and were pleased when, in 2006, he agreed to become a consultant to Rigby & Peller.

There were so many factors to be taken into consideration. As I have mentioned, Harold and David did not like to borrow money because we wanted to be in control and did not want to be working for the banks – or for anyone else for that matter. It is a very strong business ethos if you can sustain it but, as Morris pointed out, it can be limiting. The big thing for us, he suggested, was to look at where we should expand. Another shopping centre or a market town? Where do you find the more up-market 'footfall' (shopper to you and me). Shopping centres are expensive but you can get concessions; and if we were going to spread, where should we go? We hired a retail strategy group called Javelin to look at potential locations for us and they came up with Kings Road, Bow Lane, Guildford, Harrogate and Cambridge.

Slowly, slowly we advanced.

One of the things we knew from the beginning was that every time we added another Rigby & Peller store we had to change the way we operated. I cannot tell you how often I wished that my father and Uncle Jock were still around to talk to! One of the biggest changes for us was when Jill decided that she wanted to leave Rigby & Peller. She had long been involved with the media as our Marketing Director and had always had a desire to do something more in that field. Then she fell madly in love with a broadcast journalist and voiceover artist, Philip Chryssikos, who suggested that there would be a demand for a voice as expressive as Jill's in the voiceover world. How right Philip was. Jill has a wonderful voice so it has been the perfect career change for her. (And, no, he is not Jewish but he is perfect in every other way!) Philip is a deeply caring man and I don't think Jill could find anyone to love her as much. He is wonderful with Jill and lovely to our granddaughter Rachel as well, so all is good.

By now Morris was on the board of Rigby & Peller and it became obvious that the bigger we got the more warehouse space we needed – and a Head Office would not go amiss either, even though it would not necessarily add value to the business. We decided that the best strategy was for our pension fund to buy premises which Rigby & Peller could rent under a commercial lease. And that is what we did. David and Harold hit on Acton as the place to be: close to central London; good transport links; no crushing London prices. We bought a building, settled in and settled down to grow the business.

I thought life would carry on in much the same way. How wrong can you be?

CHAPTER TWELVE

Cancer.

The word alone knocks you sideways. Those two syllables explode in your brain the moment they are uttered and you cannot think about anything else. In my case the diagnosis was even more devastating personally because the c-word was preceded by the b-word – breast.

Breast health has always been a huge issue for me. I had campaigned for the Royal Marsden Early Diagnostic Unit; promoted breast awareness; held mastectomy prostheses sessions and here I was faced with having to have a mastectomy myself. It was a terrible shock and I did not expect it at all. Mind you, with hindsight, maybe I should have done.

Not long after we got married I discovered a lump in my breast, but it was benign. Over the years I had a couple more lumps removed but the tests always came back the same – non-malignant. The doctors were not concerned. It was only for my own peace of mind that I went for a yearly check-up. My consultant was a lovely man at Guys Hospital, Mr Hayward, and when he retired I would go to see another excellent breast consultant called Mr Choudray. It was very straightforward and there was never a hint that I should be concerned.

In 2007 I went for my annual check-up thinking all would be well because I had no lumps and felt fighting fit.

Mr Choudray was not as convinced as I was, however, and thought something was not quite right. It was the mammogram that confirmed there was a problem: the picture looked like I had a snow storm swirling round in my boob. Mr Choudray explained that I would have to have a mastectomy because the cancer was everywhere and not neatly contained in a lump. He put me through all sorts of other tests but the conclusion was that I had no choice.

The one element of choice that I did have, was whether or not I wanted to have immediate reconstruction using my own tissue. Of course I wanted it. It sounded like the best option by far. The procedure is called a DIEP (deep inferior epigastric perforator) flap, and is thought to be the best of all reconstruction methods. Luckily for me, I met the necessary criteria: I had enough tummy tissue; I would not need post-operative radiotherapy and I understood completely that it involved a longer operation and longer recovery time.

I would be lying if I said I wasn't terrified, but I trusted Mr Choudray, and the plastic surgeon who was going to do the reconstruction, so that is what was arranged.

It was a huge thing for Harold and the children too, and Jill says she will never forget seeing me on the morning of the operation urging Mr Choudray to, 'just get on with it because I don't have time for this'. For me, it was like the time I stood on the edge of the cliff in the Chepstow Quarry before my first abseil. Waiting, for me, equals worrying: I do not like hanging around.

As it was, I was on the operating table for ten hours. Mr Choudray removed my left breast and then Mr Chana set to and made me a new one. He took the necessary fat from my abdomen (so I got a tummy tuck at the same time); and he also saved some cartilage from my rib cage which he buried in my thigh and recovered a year later to make me a new nipple.

One of the dangers of using your own tissue for breast reconstruction is that if the blood flow is not right the tissue can die. They have to make sure all the tiny capillaries are joined up and kept open. For that reason they keep you in a hot environment after the operation because, if you get cold, there's a danger that the blood vessels can shrink. I was absolutely fine after the operation, apart from the obvious sore bits, but I thought I would die from the heat.

It took quite a long time to really recover from such an extensive procedure and it takes time to adjust to the physical difference. Once dressed, I looked exactly the same as I always did, but naked I felt I looked a little like a jigsaw that had been put together in the wrong order. But in spite of everything, the overwhelming sense was of how lucky I was. I had a new boob, made out of me, and the skill and technology that allows for that is nothing short of amazing. I also felt lucky because if I had not gone for my yearly check-up I would never have known there was problem because there was no obvious sign of one. I added up all the positives and realised there was nothing to do but thank all my lucky stars and get on with life. So that is what I did.

David and his team at Rigby & Peller were dealing with the major part of the business by this time, which allowed Harold and me more time to do what we wanted to do. In Harold's case that usually involved golf clubs, books and Tottenham Hotspur – he was a great reader and a mad Tottenham fan. I do not play golf, and prefer magazines to books, but I will watch Tottenham play if it is an important match.

I am more of a doer and particularly loved being involved in a couple of writing projects. Rosemary Conley had been a customer for years and years so I was delighted when she asked me to contribute to the underwear chapter in her book *The Secrets of Staying Young*. I didn't hesitate either when the photographer and author Gemma Levine asked me to write a chapter for her book *Go with the Flow*, which Gemma wrote in response to her own experience of breast cancer. Appropriately my chapter was about post-mastectomy fashion – a subject dear to my heart. It was also a topic that, by then, I was qualified to talk about from a personal, as well as a professional, point of view.

I also love spending time with my friends. My girlfriends have always been important to me and I love entertaining. We bought a holiday home in Spain several years ago and Harold and I have also enjoyed some memorable trips further afield. We even went to visit our former trainer, the lovely Sarah Prenter, in New Zealand. It is a stunningly beautiful country but one of the most memorable experiences was riding around Sarah's parents' farm near Hamilton in the North Island.

I have often wondered how different my life would have been had I not been set on learning to ride. It was my ambition to ride that made me determined to go to boarding school, and boarding school was the making of me. I did learn to ride at Lillesden and after I left school I took every opportunity there was to climb on a horse. Inevitably, as life got busier and work more demanding, there were fewer chances. I did, however, pass on my passion for horses to my daughter and Jill loved riding even more than I did.

One day, when Jill was still in her teens, we decided to join a hack in Richmond Park. We left Harold and Jill's boyfriend of the time at the stables and set off with a group of other riders. I had been given an enormous horse, a carthorse type of a beast that stood a full eighteen hands high. I knew that on an organised hack you are not really riding the horse; it is the horse that is taking you for a ride. You cannot make a hacking horse trot when it knows it is on a section where it always walks, and you can't make it walk if it knows you have arrived at where it should trot.

Jill and I were at the back of the group having a lovely time and a good natter. Unfortunately, I had not been warned that, when we got to the canter section of the ride, the horse I was on liked to be in front. We reached a bend in the path and, without any warning at all, my horse shot out of line, shot forward and threw me to the ground. Luckily someone who was out walking in the park raced over and ordered that I should not be moved under any circumstances. (I could not have moved anyway, I was so shocked and winded.) They called an ambulance and while I waited Jill went back to the stables to tell Harold what had happened. Eventually an ambulance arrived and they managed to get me into it. The ground was very bumpy and each bump made me scream for more gas and air. If that was not enough, at the edge of the park I had to swap ambulances because the first one broke down!

By the time we got to hospital I was in a terrible state. They cut away my clothes to discover that I had broken my shoulder blade, fractured several ribs and done something to my neck. They did what they could and sent me home. It was the most painful night of my life and the next day I insisted that Harold take me to the local hospital. They kept me in for a week, by which time I could, at least, get out of bed. My ribs mended, as did my shoulder blade, but my neck has never been right since and I have restricted movement on one side.

I didn't think the accident would put me off riding but it did. I went out a couple of times afterwards but a horse can sense when a rider is nervous and I did not enjoy myself like the days of old. Years later, the horse the Prenters saddled up for me in New Zealand was as gentle as a lamb and I had a lovely time – so lovely that when I dismounted I decided my riding days were over. 'Go out on a high, June,' I told myself. It was a surprisingly satisfying decision.

One decision that involved a lot more time and heartache was the one we took to sell the majority of our shares in our beloved Rigby & Peller. We were approached by one of our suppliers, a brilliant Belgian lingerie company called Van de Velde that made the most amazing bras. The company shared our values and we were the biggest UK stockist of their two primary brands: Prima Donna and Marie Jo.

Van de Velde had started life nearly a hundred years previously as a corsetry studio set up by a husband and wife team, Margaretha and Achiel Van de Velde, in the small town of Schellebelle in East Flanders. Over the years the company had continued to grow and in the early part of this century they set out on a major expansion programme. Their first overseas acquisitions were in 2008 in Spain when they bought the lingerie firm Eurocorset and the Spanish lingerie brand Andres Sarda. Two years later they took over the major stake in a US lingerie chain called Intimacy; and they also bought into the lingerie market in The Netherlands with the acquisition of the LinCherie chain.

It was only a matter of time before Van de Velde set their eyes on the UK and Rigby & Peller was the obvious choice. We had our headquarters in Acton and nine stores in prime locations – Knightsbridge, Mayfair, Chelsea, Bluewater Shopping Centre, Bow Lane, Guildford, Harrogate, Westfields Shopping Centre and Cambridge. David was in charge of running the business, and Jill also had shares, but Harold and I were the majority shareholders. Van de Velde had approached us a couple of times before but when they came to us in 2011 we thought it was the right time for us to think about selling – Harold was eighty, I was five years younger. We had worked very hard for a very long time.

Harold and I were in Hong Kong the day we had to make up our minds. We decided to go for it. The sale process took about six months, with endless meetings and countless questions being batted backwards and forwards between them and us and our respective solicitors. And then the deal was struck. How I wish I could have shared our success with my father and Uncle Jock. We sold 87% of our shares in Rigby & Peller for £8,000,000. I still go faint when I think about it. We had bought the company in 1982 for £20,000 (even though it was down on its uppers) and here we were, not quite thirty years later, selling it for a king's ransom. (Mind you, we had to pay a million pounds in tax almost straight away!)

It was a wonderful result for Harold and me; it was great for Jill because it guaranteed her financial security; but David took it hard. He understood why we had to accept the Van de Velde offer; he knew it was the right thing for us; but while his head appreciated the reasons for the sale, his heart was not in it at all. My darling David resented what we had decided to do. He had lived and breathed Rigby & Peller for twenty-one years and absolutely loved it. He was in his mid-forties and did not have a clue what he was going to do once his year's post-sale contract with Van de Velde ended. He agreed to stay on to oversee the transition but then David suddenly became a lingerie retailer without any lingerie to sell. It was tough for him because he had thought that Rigby & Peller would be a business he could hand on to the next generation. I have to say though that, while he may not have our genes, David is our son in every other way you can possibly imagine.

I was so relieved when, just like Harold, David's business head won the day.

David and I and Morris Miller still sit on the Rigby & Peller board in the UK and David has developed his passion for property into a new, thriving business. I have also retained my role as grantee of the Royal Warrant. Her Majesty is ninety and I am eighty, but I will continue to serve her for as long as she desires and for as long as I am able. It is a huge honour to be royal corsetiere to Queen Elizabeth II and the role is very important to me.

I also love watching the name of Rigby & Peller grow. There are still nine shops in the UK (the one in Westfields has been replaced by one in St John's Wood) and last year Van de Velde rebranded its thirteen Intimacy shops across the USA as Rigby & Peller. You will find Rigby & Peller stores in Spain, Denmark, Germany, Hong Kong and China and, in 2016, the very first Rigby & Peller franchise opened in Dubai. Jill and I went out for the opening and the directors took us out to dinner. The owner came to tell us that he had always wanted to start a luxury lingerie shop but he would not do it unless it could be Rigby & Peller. How wonderful is that?

My one regret is that, in spite of our international recognition, there is no longer our very own Rigby & Peller brand, beyond the bespoke business. Van de Velde is an enormous company and lingerie, like any other form of manufacturing, is ultimately a numbers game. When we just had the UK shops, Van de Velde decided that it was not viable for them to retain the label but we keep trying to convince them that now they have so many more Rigby & Peller boutiques…

In the meantime, I am very happy to retain my connections with the company to which Harold and I – and the children – have devoted so much of our time and energy.

I would be lying if I said I am not proud of what we have achieved. I don't think there are many retail businesses that feature in a board-game quiz question. We do: 'Who are Rigby & Peller? a. A comedy duo; b. Established gunsmiths; c. A luxury lingerie chain.'

And I have to say that I could not stop smiling several years ago when I watched an episode of *Who Wants to Be a Millionaire?*. There was a lovely young girl competing who said that, if she won, the first thing she would do would be to go to Rigby & Peller. Sadly for her she did not win, but we did arrange for her to come to the Knightsbridge shop and sent her home with a bulging goodie bag. I think it was so lovely that a young girl put us so high on her wish list and it confirmed for me that we had made it! We really made Rigby & Peller the most recognisable luxury lingerie brand in the country.

David loves telling the story that when he was once on holiday in Turkey he was talking to a group of people while pottering around in the sea. When he was asked what he did, David said he was in fashion retail. When one of the men questioned further and discovered that David was a director of Rigby & Peller he started scowling. 'Prepare to drown,' the man told David, 'you cost me a fortune every year!' And another time, in Cyprus, one woman was so excited to meet David that she rang her mother back in England to say she was having drinks with a director of Rigby & Peller and his wife.

I was absolutely thrilled when, in 2011, Rigby & Peller won the UK Lingerie Awards Independent Retailer of the Year and I was honoured with a Lifetime Achievement Award at the same ceremony. It was, I thought, the highlight of my career, but not long after we sold the bulk of our Rigby & Peller shares, my fellow trustee, Morris Miller, arranged the most wonderful, amazing surprise. Morris proposed me for an honorary doctorate in business administration at what was then Leeds Metropolitan University (now Leeds Beckett University) and the university was hugely enthusiastic about it. They had never honoured a lingerie retailer before and were not remotely put out that I do not even have an A-level to my name!

I am very used to public speaking and have done lots of talks over the years but nothing could have prepared me for speaking to the new graduates and their families on Graduation Day. I was so nervous that it was not until later, when I read the citation, that I realised lots of wonderful things had been said. 'Creativity... sound business sense... drive to succeed... industry leader...'

It was then my turn to respond. I had been told to keep it short and I did (Harold said that was a first in itself) and I thought the whole world was wonderful when I had done it. It did not bother my darling husband one bit that I had been honoured and he had not. He knows that, because of the nature of lingerie, I am the face of our business, but there has never been any question that we are a team. Any praise or accolade I get it is always, but always, for my Harold too. The greatest tragedy of our lives is that he is no longer able to recognise the fact.

My first trek for One to One: from Mount Sinai to the Promised Land, 1995.

My second trek for One to One – complete with blisters!

Princess Diana visiting Rigby & Peller in Knightsbridge, c. 1996 – she was bringing the bouquet to me! (John Kemp/All Action)

Princess Diana with Leah Gottlieb at the Gottex Headquarters in London, 1997.

The reception that Bernard Wetherill organised for us to say thank you to the then Minister of Health, Norman Fowler, for saving the Royal Marsden Early Diagnostic Unit in December 1982. (© The Press Association)

Me presenting the prize to the winner of the Rigby & Peller Stakes at the Wembley Greyhound Racing Track.

The Kenton Brothers. L–R: Harvey, Harold, Jack and Gerry.

My beautiful
children, Jill and
David, c. 2011.

July 2011, with
my Honorary
Doctorate in Business
Administration from
Leeds Metropolitan
University (now
Leeds Beckett
University). Harold
on the left and
Keith Ramsay (then
Deputy-Chair of the
Board of Governors)
on the right.
(Courtesy of Leeds
Beckett University)

Katrine Boorman's wedding basque
designed by Jasper Conran and made by
our Rigby & Peller seamstresses in 1988.

Newcastle United corset commissioned
by a loving husband for his wife!

The smile is for the bicycle I received on my seventh birthday in December 1942.

One of my favourite photos of Harold and me, taken in 2012.

Harold & me at the Van de Velde PrimaDonna Award Ceremony in 2013.

My one and only daughter, Jill, in 2016.

Jill's daughter, Rachel, with her cockapoo, Roxy.

David with his family in 2016. L–R: David, Hannah, Emily and Simona.

CHAPTER THIRTEEN

In 2012 Harold and I celebrated our Golden Wedding anniversary. Fifty wonderful years, we thought, was something to make a fuss about. We arranged to have a party at The Grove, a gorgeous hotel in Hertfordshire, invited all our close friends and family, and employed a speech writer. We thought that the occasion demanded a speech and that our speech should be like our life – a double act.

Our lovely writer did us proud and came to the house so we could rehearse what we were going to say. To make it easier for us both, she printed Harold's parts in black and mine in green. Sometimes, when we were practising, he would carry on into my part but I did not think too much of it. When he did the same thing at the party I was not amused. 'Only read the black text, Harold,' I said, in what I thought was a whisper. The whole room heard and fell about laughing because they thought it was a rehearsed thing. It was hilarious at the time, but I had the most awful, nagging feeling that it was not really funny at all.

It was not the first time that Harold had been confused. Several months earlier I had thought something was wrong – it was nothing specific, just a feeling. I made an appointment for him with our practice nurse who did a series of cognitive tests. Harold passed them all brilliantly and the nurse decided that, as my husband could count backwards from thirty without any problem at all, I was worrying unnecessarily.

Slowly, slowly, however, things got worse. Harold was always brilliant at mental arithmetic but gradually he was flummoxed by simple sums; he would forget to turn off the car when he got out of it; and there were lots of other small, silly things. Finally, I insisted my ridiculously healthy husband had to go to see a doctor. The diagnosis was made: dementia. It was a terrible shock because I knew that there was no cure and the doctor could not tell me how Harold's condition would develop, or should I say, deteriorate.

It was in January 2015 that I realised I could no longer cope on my own. We were in our house in Spain (we used to go five or six times a year) but this time Harold did not seem to recognise where we were. It took forever to convince him to get dressed in the mornings, and even longer to get him to undress at night. He is not a big man, but I am tiny, and I could not cope physically with getting him to where he needed to be at any given time. I spent the whole holiday in tears.

The children had been telling me for months that I needed help and when we came home I finally gave in and took their advice. We now have a team of Filipino carers who look after Harold for nineteen hours a day, seven days a week. I am convinced that the Filipino race is the most caring, loving race that exists. I find looking after Harold on my own impossible so I rely on Ryan Evangelista, Ron Calao, Maritess Clemente and Edson Cantos. (Edson is the one who comes to Spain with me – and he always makes sure I have the most wonderful holiday.) All the carers are so calm and patient with Harold and are amazingly loyal and reliable. They have never, ever let me down. They are all friends with each other, so if one of them can't come for any reason they sort it out between themselves. And I have always been blessed with daily women. Now I have Sue Mantle, who is wonderful too. Sue used to be a carer which, given our particular situation, is even more of a blessing. You can't have someone in your house if you are not fond of them and if they don't like you. As it is, I feel I am surrounded by friends every day.

The time I have alone with Harold, 'our time', starts at five-thirty every evening, but there is little we can do after supper other than sit and hold hands while we watch television. The greatest sadness is that Harold can no longer communicate. He might say, 'Good morning', if you say it first but, when he does try to say more, the thoughts run out before he can turn them into words. Outwardly he still looks like my Harold, and he is physically in excellent shape – personal trainer twice a week, treadmill every day – but I have no idea what is happening in his head.

If life is frustrating for Harold, he never shows it. He is such a sweetheart. Things never fazed Harold and even now he is quick to smile even in the most ridiculous situations.

David says, 'Dad lives with his condition; Mum suffers from it.' And that is true. I am constantly grateful that we can afford the care that Harold needs, but I ache for even one lucid moment with the man I adore. I miss him so much. My life has become a sort of living widowhood, so I am ever more thankful for my wonderful family and friends.

I also have time enough on my own now to reflect and think back over the years. I was talking recently about the early days with my sister, Helen, and cannot believe that her memories are so different to mine. It is as if we had completely different parents! I am always relieved when we do find memories that tally.

When Harold and I started out in business, in Brixton, we relied on the Jamaican trade, but my parents' best customers in Kilburn were Irish immigrants. I remember, when I was young, thinking that every Irish woman was called Bridie and that every Bridie had a passion for shopping at Collier's. It was a goldmine of a business and Helen remembers that too. She also remembers that our parents bought her a beautiful home when she got married and furnished it for her.

Helen and I also agree about the important role of our paternal grandmother, known always as Grandma Collier. She was a lovely woman who worked very hard to bring up her children when her husband died just before his fiftieth birthday. In turn, her children took good care of her and she lived in a gorgeous flat in St John's Wood. For as long as I can remember, Grandma Collier was at the centre of family rituals: all the women and girls in the family went to visit Grandma Collier for tea on a Tuesday; all the men and boys went on Sunday mornings. She loved cooking and would make all sorts of spoiling things for us. My personal favourite was 'lokshen' pudding and whenever I make it I always think of my lovely grandmother.

Grandma Collier died when she was ninety-one and I will never forget the rollercoaster of emotions that I rode that day. I was desperately sad because my special grandmother had died; anxious because the last time there was a death in the family it was my own darling father; excited because it was the very day that I got my engagement ring; disappointed that Grandma Collier would never get to see what the jeweller had made for me.

I don't wear my engagement ring very often these days because I have a collection of wedding rings. Over the years Harold bought me some beautiful jewellery and always indulged my passion for big rings. Silly really, but I change my wedding ring nearly every day and have done for years!

My sister-in-law, Jean, has never commented on my ring-changing habit, but were she to do so, I think she would simply dismiss it as, 'that's very June'. Jean was married to Harold's oldest brother, Harvey, and when both their children went to live in Israel they thought they should go as well. They were there for fourteen years and we often went to see them, but we knew they found life in Israel difficult. They really missed the culture of England. Harvey was in the schmutters business forever but he should have been a teacher. He was so clever, and when they came home he started giving history lectures to his local U3A (University of the Third Age) which is a wonderful organisation for retired and semi-retired people. It is not about qualifications but simply the joy of learning new things together, and Harvey absolutely loved it. Harvey died a few years ago but Jean is still an avid learner. When they came back to the UK she took up Latin and French and joined a book club.

I miss Harvey but the relative I miss most is my cousin Alan, who is probably one of my biggest regrets. During our wartime stay in Newbury, Alan and I decided one day that we were going to dig down to Australia. We must have been about five or six years old at the time and thought Australia was the best place to go to because, we thought, there would be no Germans there. We did not dare dig up my father's garden – Daddy was gardening mad and his garden was immaculate – but my uncle Harry was not so fussy so we thought his garden was the place to carry out our mission.

We started to dig and then Alan's brother, Kenny, who was quite bit older than us, decided to help. The digging proved to be quite a slow and heavy job so Kenny thought that, if we were to make it to Australia before tea, an axe would speed things up. Kenny went off to find the right tool and meanwhile Alan jumped into the hole to keep digging. When Kenny returned and swung the axe it caught Alan's head. I can still hear the screams and see poor Alan standing in Aunty Fay's bath with the blood pouring from his head. She had to take him to hospital for stitches and Kenny was told to look after me. Why my Aunty Fay thought that was a good idea I have no idea. She put me in the care of a ten-year-old who not only thought that an axe was useful, but who did not see the absurdity of trying to dig down to Australia in the first place! Luckily, I survived.

Alan and I were close all the years we were growing up. When Alan graduated he decided to be a solicitor, so Aunty Fay and Uncle Harry turned to Aunty Fay's brother, the much-adored Uncle Jock. His company solicitors were Simmons and Simmons – one of the top law firms in the country – and Alan went to train with them. Uncle Jock always used to say that the bosses at Simmons and Simmons repeatedly thanked him for making the introduction because Alan was so brilliant. Alan stayed with Simmons and Simmons for years and ended up as the senior managing partner until he retired when he was sixty.

When Alan first started in law he was so busy that we saw less and less of him. He then married an Israeli called Dalia and we hardly saw him at all. Dalia was a strange woman and I never understood why Alan married her, but he did, and they went on to have two sons and a daughter. Their eldest son, Amnon (an Israeli name apparently) was as brilliant as his father and also made a strange marriage. He went to live in the States and married a black American who was, by all accounts, a terrible social climber. Alan said she gave Amnon a hard life. Apparently, whatever Amnon did was not good enough for his wife and she eventually suggested that his life was not worth living. Tragically, Amnon agreed. He committed suicide. It was absolutely terrible and how Alan coped I do not know. I do know that Amnon's death did nothing to help Dalia's state of mind. She became more and more peculiar and Alan more and more distant. For the last twenty years of her life Dalia was a recluse and Alan spent more and more time with an old friend from Cambridge. I am sure they were more than just friends and I only wish I had taken the time to discuss it with him. I think he thought we would be horrified to learn he was homosexual. Sadly, I never took the chance to tell him that we could not have cared less.

I now know that Alan's children knew – his other son, Dan, and his daughter Edna – but I think Alan withdrew from me because he did not want me to know he was gay. I find that incredibly tragic. Alan died in 2015 and I am still upset when I think how different our relationship could have been had we had a heart-to-heart years ago.

I try hard not to dwell on the sad things of the past – or the sad things of today – because I know how lucky I am to have led a full and rich life. I am also blessed with good health.

Other than my mastectomy and the operation to screw up the joints on my right foot, I boast two lovely new knees. If you X-ray my legs and feet it's like B&Q in there and I always set off the airport security machines. One of the last times I passed through I had to be searched, yet again, and was tickled that the security woman was impressed that I was wearing a Rigby & Peller bra (of course I was). I was stunned and delighted that she recognised the brand. It has become such a well-known name. I know that is what I worked for all my business life, but it still strikes me as amazing when I find out how true it is.

I loved what we did. Lingerie is a wonderful business to be in. I love lace and prettiness and the ranges are really beautiful these days. The fabrics are utterly fantastic now too, as are the colours. I have never lost my passion for spreading the word about how important it is for women to wear a correctly fitted bra. (Nowadays the average British woman is said to be a 36D but if she were wearing the right size, I believe it would be 34DD.)

The workroom at Rigby & Peller is constantly busy, but for the average woman there is no need for made-to-measure because there is so much choice in ready-to-wear. Handmade corsetry is a dying art, which makes what our girls do particularly special. They really are experts. Apart from what they make for our devoted bespoke clients, they often make beautiful one-off garments – basques, corsets and suchlike – for various theatre and ballet companies and for brides who want something unusual. In fact one of our first Jasper Conran commissions was a bridal basque, when Jasper's brother, Tom, was marrying the actress Katrine Boorman. Jasper designed the bride's dress and those of her three bridesmaids, and described the look as 'Midsummer Dream'. He translated that into medieval, flowing gowns topped with heavily stitched and boned basques.

I love that Rigby & Peller is recognised as the place to go for special things as well as having a long-standing reputation for quality. I have had the privilege to serve some extraordinary people. I never met Margaret Thatcher but her dresser was a very nice woman. She did all Mrs Thatcher's clothes shopping and, of course, came to Rigby & Peller for lingerie. During the Blair reign I used to go to 10 Downing Street; the only time Cherie came into the shop was the day before she had to go to say goodbye to the Queen at the end of Tony's tenure. The police came in and searched the shop first and then Cherie came in. We did a fitting and she was in a fluster as to what to wear the following day, although she really was not interested in fashion at all.

Someone who is very interested in fashion is Her Majesty's current dresser, Angela Kelly. Her proper title is Personal Assistant, Advisor and Curator to Queen Elizabeth II (Jewellery, Insignia and Wardrobe). I think Angela makes the Queen look so gorgeous and has a real eye for colour. I have never been as close to her as I was to Margaret McDonald and subsequent dressers, but I do admire Angela's flair. She is a talented and lucky woman.

And I, too, am fortunate.

I have enjoyed the love and companionship of a wonderful man, and had the totally mind-blowing gift of two beautiful children who have given us three lovely grand-daughters: Hannah, Rachel and Emily mean the world to me and being a grandma is one of the most important roles in my life. I never fail to marvel that I had the chance to stand up for my principles and campaign for justice and freedom. If that were not enough, I also have had a business life that I would not swap for the world. (I am sure you will forgive me if, just sometimes, I allow myself a little flush of pride at what we have achieved.) I love that we have made Rigby & Peller a universally recognised brand.

Most of the stores look the same – give or take – but there is one thing that you will find in them all. On the wall, in every shop, is a customer quotation: 'I came in for a new bra, I left as a new woman.' It sums up what I think about Rigby & Peller. I do not know any other retail business that changes people's lives. It's gorgeous. It's amazing. How glad am I to have been part of it?

Be in no doubt, I am a very lucky woman – full stop.

THE KENTON CREED

- 85% of women are wearing the wrong size bra.
- You are your bra.
- Never buy a bra without trying it on first.
- Sizes differ depending on the brand.
- Never buy a bra without a trained fitter at your side (Rigby & Peller springs to mind).
- The benefits of underwire have never been oversold.
- Learn which style of bra suits you best (full cup, balcony etc).
- Have a selection of bras for different activities and occasions.
- Some bras are better for the bedroom than the boardroom.
- Once a 34B not always a 34B – your size and shape change constantly.
- Be breast aware – check your boobs regularly.*
- Bra gift vouchers make wonderful presents (Rigby & Peller springs to mind again, but you wouldn't expect anything else would you?).

* *Breast Cancer Now estimates that one in eight women will be diagnosed with breast cancer during their lifetime. Early diagnosis leads to early treatment leads to better chances of survival.*

GLOSSARY

I have used several words and expressions throughout the book that you may not be familiar with, so I thought a little explanation might be helpful.

Bar mitzvah: literally 'son of the commandment' in Hebrew. When a Jewish boy turns thirteen he is considered old enough to observe religious principles. There is a ceremony and, usually, a party.

Bat mitzvah: literally 'daughter of the commandment'. The same as above, but a girl is considered to reach maturity at the age of twelve.

Büstenhalter: the German word for bra.

Challah: plaited bread eaten on the Sabbath and Jewish holidays.

Chutzpah: audacity or self-confidence.

Coch-lefel: a mixing spoon used for cooking.

Dvar Torah: a presentation on a Jewish religious text.

Frum: religious.

Frumpence: a variation of 'flumpence', meaning a small or derisory amount.

Kibbutz: a settlement in Israel where all property is communally owned.

Kiddush: literally 'sanctification'. It is a blessing recited over wine at the start of the Sabbath on Friday night and also on Jewish holidays.

Lokshen: Jewish noodles which look a little like skinny macaroni.

Matzoh: unleavened bread.

Matzoh pudding: slang for a fuss or a palaver.

Moshav: a collective settlement where land and tools are shared rather than co-operatively owned.

Pesach: Passover. One of the main Jewish festivals of the year. It is a commemoration and celebration of the Israelites' liberation from slavery in Egypt, as told in the Book of Exodus.

Schlep: a tedious journey.

Schmutters: clothing. The 'schmutters business' is a variation on the 'rag trade'.

Shabbat: the Jewish word for the Sabbath.

Shofar: a horn made out of ram's horn used on various religious occasions.

Siddur: a Jewish prayer book.

Torah: the first five books of the Jewish Bible.

Yahrzeit: the anniversary of a death, particularly that of a parent.